# Asking Big Questions

# Asking Big Questions

Targeting a Christian Apologetics Film
Series Using Market Research

Grenville J. R. Kent

WIPF & STOCK · Eugene, Oregon

ASKING BIG QUESTIONS
Targeting a Christian Apologetics Film Series Using Market Research

Copyright © 2014 Grenville Kent. All rights reserved. Except for brief quotations in critical publications or reviews, no part of this book may be reproduced in any manner without prior written permission from the publisher. Write: Permissions, Wipf and Stock Publishers, 199 W. 8th Ave., Suite 3, Eugene, OR 97401.

Wipf and Stock
An Imprint of Wipf and Stock Publishers
199 W. 8th Ave., Suite 3
EUGENE, OR 97401

www.wipfandstock.com

ISBN 13: 978-1-62564-490-9

Manufactured in the U.S.A. 06/18/2014

To Carla, with love.

And for Zoe, Marcus, Ethan, Thomas, Jeremy and Zara,
in the hope that they will be eternally curious
(Exod 13:14; Deut 6:20).

And in memory of James Winston Kent and
all those chairlift conversations.

# Contents

*Preface* | ix
*Acknowledgements* | xi

1 Introduction | 1

2 Theological Background | 17

3 Literature Review | 52

4 Qualitative Research and Interpretation | 74

5 Conclusion | 148

*Bibliography* | 153
*Subject Index* | 165
*Author Index* | 169

# Preface

If you could make documentaries giving evidence for Christian faith, what should they say and how should they say it?

My current ministry task involves writing and producing a film series for apologetics, and so I conducted research to examine attitudes to God in one demographic in Sydney: the young, educated, urban segment described by market researchers Jill Caldwell and Christopher Brown as the "Balmain Tribe." This present study is based on a research project submitted to the Australian College of Theology as part of a Doctor of Ministry in 2012.

Theologically, it is modelled on Paul's Athenian mission (Acts 17:16–34), particularly its listening, dialogical approach to various demographics and its focus on one particular social grouping.

Thirteen in-depth interviews were conducted with people from the Balmain tribe to ask which experiences, intuitions, perceptions, and lines of argument tend to incline them toward a belief in a personal God, and which incline them away. They generally felt intuitive and emotional attraction to the notion of God, but were less comfortable with that intellectually. They were also asked the relative strength and importance of these factors; how they fit them together; and how important and urgent this question has been at various times in their lives. God was not a priority for most, even in crisis.

They were then reminded of some classic arguments for and against the existence of a personal God, and asked to comment on how convincing they found these.

These findings were analyzed and applied to Christian apologetics by considering which are "common ground" areas with Christianity, and which areas may be objections to Christianity (or their current view of it), and how *Big Questions* could build on the former and address the latter. This was relevant to the question of what topics should be included, and how they should and should not be addressed.

It was concluded that these findings helped to inform and fine-tune apologetic approaches to this demographic, and that other researchers could apply this model to other demographics.

# Acknowledgements

> Committees are by nature timid, based on the premise of safety in numbers, content to survive, rather than take risks and move independently ahead. Independence, then, has always been the attitude at Porsche. To do not what is expected, but to do what we feel is right...
>
> Committees lead to creations that have no soul, no clear identity—this is why no Porsche will ever be created by a committee, but by a handful of people who know what a Porsche is.
>
> —PROF. FERDINAND PORSCHE[1]

I wouldn't claim *Big Questions* is a Porsche quality film series, but I am grateful to Pastors Chester Stanley and Graeme Christian for being my handful of people. Thanks immensely for seeing the vision from the beginning and for wise, kind mentoring.

My name is on the front of this book, but many other people contributed to it, especially the savvy market researchers whose work is so central to this study, and who added questions, insights and language to my initial curiosity: to Jill Caldwell at Windshift, and to Mark McCrindle, Claire Madden and Hester Kahei at

---

1. Senn, "Moment with Ferry Porsche," *Porsche Panorama*, www.pca.org/Panorama/AMomentwithFerryPorsche.aspx.

## Acknowledgements

McCrindle Research. Thanks to Tina Guan and to Windshift for diagrams and graphics.

Marcia and Graeme Christian helped to frame questions and tamed a pile of 631 surveys. Pastor Ken Vogel gave input on survey design, and Pastor Anthony MacPherson added insights to the key findings. Cathy McDonald—ever hungry for more data about people—was a great teammate in managing the first study reported here.

At Morling College, Rev Dr Phill Marshall was a deeply calm and encouraging supervisor, and Rev Dr Graham Hill's grasp of detail helped especially during the submission process. My enthusiasm for apologetics was built by logical, imaginative classes with Rev. Steve Clarke and Rev. Dr. Ross Clifford.

Thanks to my examiners, Professor Neil Ormerod of Australian Catholic University, Dr. Lars Dahle of Gimlekollen School of Journalism and Communication in Norway, and Dr. Philip Hughes of Christian Research Association in Melbourne, for their critical feedback and encouragement.

I am immensely grateful to Carla, who has backed the *Big Questions* project with endless encouragement and humour and a marathon work ethic. What a godsend you are to me.

And first and last God. For a minute there I thought I was whizzing round a random, entropic universe in distorted circles on this little mudball, unparented, trying to pack as much pleasure and purpose into my selfish little life as possible before sleeping the big sleep, but you impatiently and surprisingly spoke to me via sharp, colourful, generous characters, and cut through the bozone layer around my head with love and truth and good news. Thank you, forever and a day. Help me to pass on the favor.

# 1

## Introduction

WHAT DO AUSTRALIANS THINK about God, and why? What factors—logical, emotional, experiential, intuitive—incline them toward belief and what toward unbelief? How do they weigh these factors, and balance them if they compete? Why do many seem to be "swing voters" in the unsure middle on this question, sitting comfortably on the fence, unmotivated to move far either way? In what areas do they share common ground with Christianity? What are their objections to Christian belief and practice, and their misunderstandings of Christianity? What apologetical approaches would make most sense to them? What media products do they enjoy and trust? And how should these insights influence apologetics—specifically, an apologetics-based film series?

These are questions that have fascinated me in the twenty-seven years since I became a Christian (thanks largely to apologetic outreach or thoughtful "persuasive evangelism"). When making outreach presentations to live audiences, I often ask them to list reasons why people do or do not believe in God, noting these on a whiteboard and discussing each in turn. I must have done this hundreds of times over the years, which served as some kind of market research.

These questions are also directly relevant to my current ministry focus as a writer-producer of an outreach film series called

*Big Questions*. It aims to do unapologetic apologetics—and yes, I would like a less ambiguous title: Christian evidences? Persuasive evangelism? These thirteen films will make the case for the veracity and usefulness of Christianity and the Bible. Specifically, this project forms a polite response to the well-publicized and influential New Atheism of Richard Dawkins, Daniel Dennett, Christopher Hitchens, Sam Harris, Michel Onfray, and the like, and takes up many of their arguments.

The brief positioning statement (or "elevator pitch") of *Big Questions* is:

> An evangelistic film series for the urban, thinking person in a globalised culture, to persuade them entertainingly (respecting their intelligence) in their preferred media that God exists and is worth knowing through Jesus.[1]

## *Big Questions*: A Brief History

Filmmaker Marcus Gillezeau describes a cyclical model of film production, beginning with concept (generating creative ideas), then development (refining the idea, selecting key personnel), financing, pre-production (planning the shoot), production, post-production (editing and music), marketing, distribution and, as a result of all this, generating fresh concepts and beginning the process again.[2] This research project began at the end of the concept stage and overlapped development. I am not coming to it *tabula rasa*, because research rarely works like that, and nor do I expect audiences to tell me my message or product: who could have market researched the idea of the Internet in 1985? Yet I regard this research as part of the creative development process, sensing the value of testing ideas and hypotheses on real people in a formal way with feedback and peer review, as an attempt to be more objective rather than "precious" about my ideas. This research was performed while I still had time to re-script, or indeed to replace entire episodes if the research suggested the topic is inappropriate for some reason. Previous to

---

1. Kent, *Big Questions Prospectus*, 12.
2. Gillezeau, *Hands On*.

the project reported in this thesis, there were also surveys of young Christians in tertiary education (sample size c. 400) and of Christian ministers (sample size c. 90), which were coordinated by Graeme Christian, one of the Executive Producers of *Big Questions*, but which are not fully reported here.

I have been dreaming for about fifteen years of doing a project like this. In 2008 I took long service leave and went on a Billy Graham-style mission team to Russia, where I had some free time to think and pray. I reread the book of Acts, and saw particular relevance in Acts 17, as I will explain in the next chapter. I wrote feverishly: concepts, approaches, initial drafts for scripts, a basic marketing plan. This was my concept stage. I then came home and pitched the *Big Questions* concept to Christian philanthropists and to senior church executives. The essence of the pitch was to draw a three-tiered pyramid on the lunch napkin or whiteboard, asking them to imagine their faith as a pyramid. The base level was to do with the question "Is there a God?," and the blocks were classic arguments for and against theism. The second level up said, "Which God?," and here were arguments for Jesus and the Bible (though not arguments against other religions). The highest level was called "How do I relate to God?," and considered devotional questions and denominational distinctives. I then asked three questions. First, at which level were most Australians a generation or two ago? They would say, "Level three." Second, at which level are most young, educated Australians today? They would answer, "Level one." Third, I would ask where their church currently spends most of its energy and money and media resources. They would answer immediately, "Level three!" and their faces would show that they had seen the problem clearly.

We received development funding for a first script and then, after audience testing, a budget to produce it as a pilot episode. I am fairly conservative about claims of providence, but I experienced clear examples of God's leading. We wanted access to a Qantas A380, but senior journalists and well-connected Qantas staff told us the company could not afford to let their half-billion-dollar asset sit idle while we filmed it. Eventually I discovered a work colleague was married to the head of maintenance, and we were given permission to film while the big bird was being serviced, as long as we could find our own A380 pilot. I then discovered one attending my local church. Involvement from Qantas helped land us permission to film at the Airbus factory, and we arrived in France with a film crew only to find our trip arranger had entered a coma. Somehow we reconstructed our schedule at the last possible minute and missed nothing. Providences like these were very encouraging that we were going down the right path. Our first film was played to a number of small test audiences (fewer than 30 people), who liked it somewhat but found it unclear and boring at certain points. I was emotionally close to the project, but this feedback helped bring some objectivity and distance, and their comments clarified a number of things and sent me enthusiastically to the edit room for a recut. The recut version received immeasurably better responses from groups, and was then sent to two independent companies, a social researcher and a market researcher. The results from these larger studies were most encouraging, and the commissioning editor of Channel 7 expressed an interest in potentially screening a short series of the films. This pilot episode can be viewed at BigQuestions.com.

On the strength of this, we applied for funding for the entire series of thirteen films (a television season).

Part of the motive for this research was to seek some level of objectivity on this project, as I was writer and producer. I recognize the danger of being biased and defensive about my ideas, and the need for peer review and audience feedback. For one example, I sensed that involving my young son Marcus as junior co-presenter would work well, but I did not want parental fondness to write policy, and so our early surveys specifically asked about the issue. A large majority say that the child presenter made the content seem easier to understand and removed any sting from the debate, but that the child should not present information like he had done briefly in episode 1: he should merely ask questions and function as the voice of curiosity. I noted both the encouragement and the correction for future episodes.

*Introduction*

The marketing and distribution plan, broadly speaking, is to contract a distribution company to sell the documentary series to TV channels globally (including in translation), and to sell it as home DVD. We intend to maximize distribution rather than profit since our backers are happy to consider their capital investment a gift, because they believe in giving the gospel away for free. We will offer non-exclusive licences because we want church groups (in fact, any groups who want it) to use it on DVD. After twelve to twenty-four months we will give it away on the Internet, offering free downloads for iPod and various other formats, and using viral marketing via e-mail, MySpace, and Facebook. (We may charge for high-resolution downloads, as a way of funding the next series.) We also hope to route people to evangelistic churches for follow-up, which will mean working on a global contact list for every city.

Here in Australia, we have tested an approach to seminar evangelism. A church gives away ten thousand copies of a documentary in their area (at about fifty cents per copy), and advertises a seminar with the presenter tackling questions like the existence of God or the problem of suffering. Our pilot program in Brisbane in the winter of 2010 drew a number of non-Christians, many of whom were friends of Christians and some of whom just turned up, and who were then invited to follow-up seminars exploring Christianity.

Recognizing a range of views within church circles, I am trying to be as inclusive as I can, especially when discussing basic theism. For example, in discussing cosmology I have tried to avoid questions of the big bang (see the discussion in the Cosmological Argument section of chap. 4) and simply look at fine tuning. As much as possible, I would like to avoid contention and affirm what all sides can affirm. For example, in addressing the question of suffering, which I find is the most commonly raised objection to theism, I will use the Christian Free Will Defense pioneered by Alvin Plantinga. Some people and churches will not favor that approach, but I hope that they can still use other films in the series.

## Project Description: Target Audience

Our target audience is urban young adults, with a skew to education.

I have noticed that producers of Christian outreach projects often feel reluctant to define a target audience too closely because it can feel like we are excluding other groups and narrowing the universal call of the gospel. I will argue below that Paul in Athens (and Luke in writing Acts) was keenly aware of the needs of various audiences, and unafraid to target them. Defining a target need not mean excluding anyone who may be interested; secondary targets can also benefit, sometimes even accidentally.

Our market segmentation is based on the "Eight Tribes" concept. This is a values-based segmentation of people in Anglo-Saxon societies, based on the inherited class structures and the social distinctions that people sense and construct about themselves and each other. It was pioneered by Jill Caldwell and Christopher Brown[3] and is now being applied to Australian society in consultancies to leading corporates. It uses the word *tribes* in a loose and popular sense rather than as a careful sociological definition: obviously each tribe will have considerable variety within it. As an introductory snapshot, here is Caldwell and Brown's segmentation of Australian society:

3. Caldwell and Brown, *Eight Tribes*.

*Introduction*

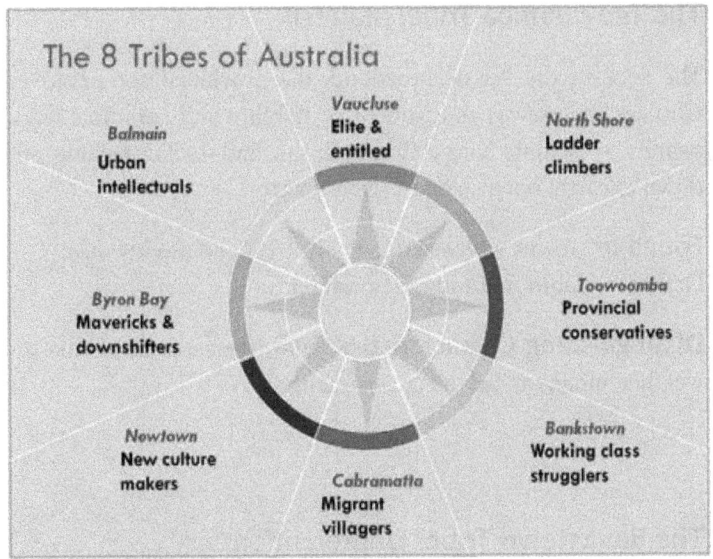

A brief description of the tribes follows:[4]

### The North Shore Tribe: Achieving

The ambitious, hard-working, heavily mortgaged inhabitants of the great suburban jungle for whom looking good and keeping up appearances are fundamentally important. They survive in the jungle by constantly moving ahead, up through the ranks of job, car, house, street, and suburb.

**Found In:** Commuter suburbs, gathering in offices, gyms and shopping malls.

**Distinguishing Characteristics:** New cars, new toys, long commutes, tropical resort holidays, stress-related health issues.

---

4. Adapted by Grenville Kent from Caldwell and Brown, *Eight Tribes*, from www.8tribes.co.nz, and from discussions with Jill Caldwell. It is recognized that these are broad descriptors only, and that many exceptions and nuances exist.

### The Toowoomba Tribe: Staunch

The tribe of the Aussie heartland, the provincial conservatives, who see themselves as a source of stability and common sense, bearers of ongoing connection with the land—solid, reliable, and down to earth, but also deceptively smart.

**Found In:** Towns with a single main street and muddy utes. Gather in clubrooms and memorial halls.

**Distinguishing Characteristics:** Down-to-earth-ness, talks of weather, moans about the government.

### The Bankstown Tribe: Unpretentious

Urban working people who disdain "wankers" and define themselves by their unwillingness to think of themselves as better than their mates—the classic "housing commission and keg" Aussies.

**Found In:** Suburbs and towns with concentrations of car-yards, supermarkets, and sports grounds.

**Distinguishing Characteristics:** Shift work, blue overalls, budgets.

### The Cabramatta/Campbelltown Tribe: Community

Urban, often immigrant, community-minded people from village cultures in Asia, Europe, or the Pacific, where family is paramount and church is likely to play a central social role, or if not church then another club-based group. The sense of belonging and support structures are very strong, as is the pressure to "do the right thing" and uphold appearances.

**Found In:** Areas with concentrations of state housing.

**Distinguishing Characteristics:** Large social gatherings, infectious laughter, colorful rituals, feasts.

## The Newtown Tribe: Avant-Garde

A transitional tribe for young alternative Aussies on the cutting edge of cool, where "new" is the greatest virtue, being labeled mainstream the greatest fear, and self-expression the great preoccupation. The Newtown Street tribe is the edge from which many trends and fashions emerge—in the 80s it was the vanguard of espresso; in the 90s, of body piercing and tattoos.

**Found In:** Bohemian zones in central areas of main cities, at the coolest gigs, at art schools and universities.

**Distinguishing Characteristics:** Looks weird, likes looking weird.

## The Byron Bay Tribe: Free Spirited

The independent spirits who value the ability to live a life according to their own priorities, not the consumerist pressures for material aggrandizement. They tend to be highly sensate and internally focused—hedonists, or spiritual journeyers, fitness fanatics or adrenaline junkies. Many Aussies join the Byron Bay tribe for three weeks at Christmas.

**Found In:** Laid-back suburbs on the wild side of town, or small settlements in beautiful places.

**Distinguishing Characteristics:** Old station wagons, stacks of firewood, mismatched possessions.

Asking Big Questions

### The Balmain Tribe: Intellectual

The highly educated intelligentsia who value ideas above material things and intellectualize every element of their lives. Their most prized possession is a painting by the artist of the moment, they frequent film festivals, secretly wish they had more gay, Muslim, and aboriginal friends, feel guilty about discussing property values, and deep down are uneasy about their passion for rugby (or League).

**Found In:** Suddenly fashionable ex-working-class suburbs. Large groups will gather at bohemian inner city cafes, intellectual bookshops, ethnic cultural events and film festivals.

**Distinguishing Characteristics:** Prefers to be "challenged" rather than entertained, seeks out authentic experiences, blushes when talking about property values.

### The Vaucluse Tribe: Entitled

The round-vowelled children of privilege for whom breeding is the greatest virtue, manners really do make a difference, money is great if it's old but crass if it's new, and the school you went to defines the rest of your life.

**Found In:** Leafy enclaves of the elite old city suburbs and in leafy corners of provincial towns with old sheep-grazier traditions.

**Distinguishing Characteristics:** Rounded vowels, meticulous manners.

*Introduction*

Spiritual beliefs have a key defining role in two tribes: Cabramatta/Campbelltown, where migrants bring their strong sense of community usually based around religion, and Byron Bay, where post-materialist individualists create their own systems of belief, often linked with nature. Yet other tribes have their own distinctive take on spiritual values, in ways that reflect their life values. The anti-intellectual approach of Bankstown tribe and the homespun conservatism of the Toowoomba tribe have some overlap. Vaucluse (elite) and Newtown (culture-makers) are numerically small but influential, especially in social trends and media, though our pilot study could not access people from Vaucluse, perhaps because our payment was well below their hourly rate—a common problem in researching the elite. Our initial pilot study of attitudes to God and to religion generated the following visual summary of findings:

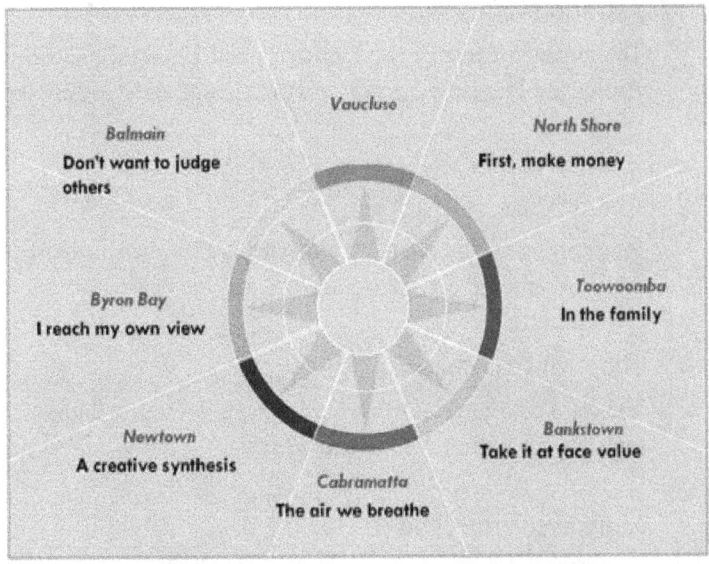

The Balmain tribe has been chosen as the target audience of the *Big Questions* project. This is partly because they are the tribe I understand best, where many of my friends are, and where some of my best ministry experiences have been. Their intellectualism seems to suggest they would be a good audience for apologetics, since they could be encouraged to consider the rational case for Christianity, and the value they place on ethics and virtue suggests they may consider Christian values and, in turn, the worldview that produces them. All in all, they seem like a prime target audience for a persuasive approach to Christianity.

## Project Description: Topic Outline

The following topics are slated for production:

1. **Baby, Baby**
   The Argument from Design in embryology, also briefly covering suffering in nature. (Ps 139:16)

2. **Astronomical!**
   The argument from Fine-Tuning in the Universe / Cosmic Anthropic Principle and the classic Cosmologic Argument. (Psalm 19)

3. **Antarctic Ice**
   Fine-tuning in the chemistry of water, as shown in climate systems centered on Antarctica.

4. **The Artificial Albatross**
   The classic Argument from Design, applied to the flight systems of an albatross. (Job 39:26–30)

5. **Monkeys Wrote This**
   The classic Argument from Design, applied to DNA using the language analogy.

*Introduction*

6. Me, Robot?
   The Argument from Consciousness, comparing a child to a super-robot.

7. Why Should I Care?
   The moral argument, applied to child sex trafficking.

8. Sex and Spirit
   Christian values improve life, and best describe the whole human being (including the soul).

9. God, why suffering?
   Answering the classic Problem of Evil with the Christian Free Will Defense.

10. O, Jerusalem
    An introduction to Messianic prophecy (Daniel 9).

11. Life after Death—Really?
    A look at Epicureanism and Christianity.

12. Is Jesus History?
    A critical examination of the historicity of Jesus, and the transmission of the NT documents.

13. Doubting Thomas
    A critical look at the resurrection of Jesus.

These could of course change in response to further research.

A previous version included an episode titled "If God Is Dead," and interviewed atheists about the implications of secular materialism: no purpose, no soul, no love above the biochemical, likely no afterlife, etc. The idea was to do what Francis Schaeffer

13

## Asking Big Questions

called "taking the roof off"[5] to reveal the real-life implications of secular ideas. However, audiences found it a depressing topic, and thought we were being too negative in criticizing someone else's view. I had also been planning to treat the issue of sexuality, particularly because the global clergy abuse scandal came up so often in question time after my public talks. And so we substituted episode 8.

### Project Description: Overall Approach

Our approach is to be entertainingly persuasive. Our first task is to capture people's attention. The documentary medium, while traditionally informational and formal and "telling" in style, has more recently been used in a "new age" way to raise questions, and in a comedic way: witness Michael Moore or the globally high-rating *Top Gear*. As a preacher and theologian used to words and abstract theology, I note that the film medium runs on visuals, physical action, and the concrete to illustrate the abstract and propositional. We also aim to raise questions rather than to preach or tell.

I also plan to release a book with the main content in a slightly more dense form, reasoning that this suits those who prefer to read.

### Research Question(s)

To do the best job possible of reaching the Balmain Tribe, I need to ask: what factors incline them toward belief in (the Christian) God, what factors incline them away, and how do they balance them? I will then try to address these factors in the film series, informed by any learning about their existing views on these questions.

I can break these down into the following questions:

---

5. To my knowledge, Schaeffer does not use the term in print, but his use of it is noted by his student William Edgar, "Two Christian Warriors," 59.

- What thoughts, intuitions, experiences, perceptions and lines of argument incline you to a belief in a personal God? (Keeping it holistic rather than intellectual only.)
- What thoughts, intuitions, experiences, perceptions and lines of argument incline you away from a belief in a personal God?
- What is the relative strength of these factors?
- How do you balance them out / fit them all together? E.g., the personal and the philosophical.
- How important do you find the question of God's existence? Has this changed at various times in your life? Why?
- What do you see as your purpose in life? How did you arrive at this?
- What helps you through crisis and uncertainty? (I'm really asking: What fills the traditional place of religion in your life?)
- What characteristics would you associate with people who believe or don't believe in God? For example, how would you finish these sentences: "Most believers are…" "Most nonbelievers are…" (I'm really asking: Do belief and non-belief in God make a difference to how people live?)

These will be expanded into a questionnaire in chapter 4.

## Research Objective

My aim is to apply these findings to the *Big Questions* films, an applied apologetics project and, more broadly, to Christian evangelism / apologetics / mission.

Specifically, I would like to know:

a. Which beliefs / thoughts / intuitions / ethical views do people already hold in common with Christianity, and can work as bridges to it?

b. Which beliefs / thoughts / intuitions / experiences / ethical views do they hold in opposition to Christianity. Are these objections to Christianity or only their *current* view of Christianity?

c. How we can build on (a) and credibly address (b).

d. Any other insights about how we can target (and position) the Christian message to this demographic.

This project will describe the theological impetus behind the *Big Questions* project (chapter 2), and then summarize key existing research into Australian spirituality (chapter 3), before moving to its own research and application of key findings to the project (chapter 4), and offering conclusions (chapter 5).

# 2

## Theological Background

> Only familiarity blinds us to nature's marvels.
>
> —BALBUS[1]

THIS CHAPTER DESCRIBES THE biblical paradigm that has motivated and informed the *Big Questions* project. It is a media production using apologetics, which can be defined as "the rational justification of Christian truth claims over against relevant questions, objections and alternatives."[2]

Acts 17 has long inspired apologists,[3] evangelists, and missionaries. Rather than addressing Israel as so much of biblical

---

1. Cicero, *De natura deorum II.* 95, 76–80, 81–97, 98–153, 162, cited in Winter, "Introducing the Athenians to God," 51.
2. Dahle, "Acts 17:16–34," *Tyndale Bulletin*, 313.
3. For example, see Bolt, "New Testament Apologetics," 487–90; Carson, *Gagging of God*, 496–505; Clark and Geisler, *Apologetics in the New Age*, 7; Cook, *Blind Alley Beliefs*, 171–74; Charles, "Engaging the (Neo)Pagan Mind," 47–62; DiCello, "Athenian Challenge"; Zeolla, "Paul in Athens"; Dyrness, *Christian Apologetics in a World Community*, 25; Geisler, *Baker Encyclopedia of Christian Apologetics*, 39; Geisler and Brooks, *When Skeptics Ask*, 14; Guinness, *Fit Bodies—Fat Minds*, 350, 358; McGrath, "Biblical Models for Apologetics, Parts 1–4"; McGrath and Green; *Springboard for Faith*, 77–80; Mayers, *Balanced Apologetics*, 164–71; Montgomery, *Faith Founded on Fact*, 36–42; Netland, "Apologetics, Worldviews, and the Problem of Neutral Criteria."

## Asking Big Questions

revelation does, this narrative shows the apostle to the Gentiles seeking to understand various target audiences and adapting his approach accordingly. Seeing idolatry in Athens, he begins in the synagogue with Jews and god-fearers, as he often did in cities,[4] but also offers speeches and discussions in the *agora* to whoever passes by, and also produces polished advocacy in the rarefied atmosphere of the Areopagus with leading thinkers and policy-makers. In marketing terms, Paul segments the market, chooses his target segments (though the Areopagites chose him), and then positions himself to reach each segment or demographic specifically. Paul also models a willingness to engage and critique the culture(s) of Athens, and so a rabbi-turned-Christian evangelist examines idols, the very things that have stirred him up, and quotes Greek poetry, finding what common ground he can. "Paul is seen operating at his apologetic best, engaged in moral discourse with the intellectual and cultural elite of his day," impressively able to "clothe biblical revelation in a cultured and relevant argument to his pagan contemporaries" and to "contextualize."[5] Despite the passing of almost two millennia, gospel communicators find connections with Paul's mission:

> The closest parallel to our own situation is Paul's encounter with paganism in Acts 17. In modern western culture, few have any knowledge of the biblical background assumed in the apostolic preaching to the Jews. But those who wish to communicate the gospel to our own generation would do well to recover and apply those same perspectives, even as Paul does embryonically in Acts 17.[6]

---

57; Prior, *Gospel in a Pagan Society*, 176–82; Proctor, "Gospel from Athens," 69–72; Thornton, "Paul's Apologetic at Athens," 2–22. Particularly presuppositionalist approaches include: Van Til, *Paul at Athens*; Oliphint, *Battle Belongs to the Lord*, 143–73; and Bahnsen, *Always Ready*, 235–76.

4. Gray, "Implied Audiences," 208, sees a pattern: Pisidian Antioch (13:13–41), Iconium (14:1–7), Thessalonica (17:1–9), Berea (17:10–14), Ephesus (19:8–20). Cf. Conzelmann, "Address," 219.

5. Charles, "Engaging," 53, 54.

6. Peterson, "Resurrection Apologetics," 55.

Paul's speech has been called the "greatest missionary document in the New Testament,"[7] "an object lesson in apologetics,"[8] "a classic of intercultural communication applicable to our own increasingly pluralistic world,"[9] an example "in building bridges where possible without shirking the necessity of dialogue on points of basic disagreement, while seeking to meet those issues where the questioner is, in his own ground and terminology."[10]

## A Failed Experiment?

Some scholars have argued that Paul's Areopagus speech was unsuccessful and recorded by Luke largely as an example of what does not work.[11] For them, Paul had been "too intellectual," or "had not preached the gospel," and a lack of conversions led him to renounce the intellectual approach and "know nothing but Jesus Christ, and him crucified" (1 Cor 2:2).[12] There is no question that Athens was inhospitable to the gospel. We have no epistle to the Athenians, so it seems no major church was founded immediately,[13] however Paul probably sowed for others to reap. It seems clear that Paul did follow a different strategy in Corinth. Writing "some four years later," Paul emphasizes the simplicity of the gospel he presented, and yet this is not necessarily a categorical denial of "the intellectual approach," but could be an ironic recognition of the "shallow intellectualism of the Corinthians," not wanting to "give them a Christianity diluted with pseudo-philosophical ideas."[14] Corinth was a different city, a trading center rather than a "university town,"

---

7. Deissman, *Light from the Ancient East*, 384.
8. McGrath, *Bridge-Building*, 49.
9. Hemer, "Speeches of Acts," 255.
10. Ibid., 247.
11. E.g. Ramsay, *St. Paul the Traveller*, 252; Dibelius, *Studies in the Acts of the Apostles*, 63.
12. Stott, *Contemporary Christian*, 60, argues against this view.
13. McGrath, *NIV Bible Companion*, 323.
14. Blaiklock, "Areopagus Address," 190.

and here the major segment of people would not be interested in elaborate philosophical argument.

One could say that Paul switched from targeting a niche audience to a mass audience. Contemporary marketing may offer a parallel. Audi's advertising slogan is *Vorsprung durch Technik*.[15] Audi's target audience is the well-heeled, well-educated AB demographic, and their slogan compliments the reader who can translate it, subtly suggesting they belong to a small, special group of cognoscenti, while people who don't understand can be left wondering. This is niche marketing. Compare the slogan for Holden Special Vehicles: "I just want one." This is simple, visceral, unsophisticated, and adapted to an affluent blue-collar "tradie" market, much more a mass audience. In raw numbers, sales to a niche audience are smaller than those to a mass market, which may help explain Paul's disappointingly small numbers in Athens.

Paul wrote to the Corinthians that he became "all things to all people so that by all means he might save *some*" (1 Cor 9:22). The rhetorical repetition conditions the reader to expect him to conclude by saying "all," but in honesty Paul can only write "some." In Corinth he challenged the "wisdom" which "knew not God" (cf. 1 Cor 1:18—2:16), just as he had done in a more sophisticated way in Athens.[16]

Stott has written, "What Paul renounced in Corinth was not the biblical doctrine of God as Creator, Lord and Judge, but the wisdom of the world and the rhetoric of the Greeks."[17] Winter cites a convention in Roman colonies that an orator was supposed to speak on a topic chosen by the audience, and his speech needed to be "a model of sophisticated oratory."[18] Aristotle, in his classic *Rhetoric*, had outlined three proofs of persuasion:

> Of the modes of persuasion furnished by the spoken word there are three kinds...Persuasion is achieved by the speaker's *personal character* when the speech is so

15. Meaning "progress through technology."
16. Wright, "Paul's Purpose at Athens," 12.
17. Stott, *Message of Acts*, 290.
18. Winter, "Introducing the Athenians to God," 58.

spoken as to make us think him credible...Secondly, persuasion may come through the hearers, when the *speech stirs their emotions*...Thirdly, persuasion is effected through the *speech itself* when we have proved a truth or an apparent truth by means of the persuasive arguments suitable to the case in question.[19]

Paul's Athens speech was highly polished, and its rhetorical structure[20] and use of assonance, alliteration, and paronomasia[21] have been analyzed. In Corinth, Paul "rejected this as he did not want the hearers" faith to be placed in the wisdom of the speaker but in the power of God" (cf. 1 Cor 2:2; 5:1).[22]

Of course, the results are mixed: some mock or procrastinate. "God's call to repentance, while directed at all irrespective of nation, will be ignored more often than not."[23] This is not purely an intellectual matter: the biblical apologist has to contend also with the work of Satan.[24] And Acts describes the apostles suffering hardships in other cities.

Yet was Athens a failure? Dionysius the Areopagite and Damaris and "some others" (Acts 17:34) would not have said so. Paul may have sown more than reaped in Athens, but his success is measured by people who converted to the gospel and who could look forward to an eternity of bliss after death—surely an achievement of infinite worth. If this narrative warns against anything, it is "a warning to those who, in misguided moments, have seen a virtue in crudity, and a loyalty to truth in a disrespect for the views, the habits of thought, and the attitudes of intelligent people who fail in all points to follow them." Paul did not shy away from the offence of the cross, but the confrontation came after courteous,

---

19. Aristotle, *Rhetoric*, 7.
20. See Dahle, "Acts 17:16–34," PhD diss., 76.
21. See Hemer, "Speeches of Acts," 256n47.
22. Winter, "Introducing the Athenians to God," 59.
23. Gray, "Implied Audiences," 218.
24. As Whitcomb points out in "Contemporary Apologetics."

rational and patient persuasion, and with "tolerance that is not incompatible with earnestness."[25]

So we can agree with Dahle that Luke intends the story to function "*both* in order to confirm the truth-value of the Christian faith *and* to provide [Christians] with apologetical tools and models for reaching outsiders."[26]

## Segmenting the Market: Different Audiences

The narratives in Acts are rich in descriptions of cultures and subcultures.[27] This may be because Luke takes seriously Christ's commission to take the good news to all nations. Acts regularly pays close attention to the background of hearers, and strategically records speeches to key audiences:[28] Jewish (2:14–36; 3:12–26; 4:8–12; 5:29–32; 10:34–43; 13:16–41), Christian (20:17–35), and pagan: both a brief speech to a mass audience in Lystra (14:15–17), and an oration for sophisticated pagans in the cultural and intellectual capital (17:16–34).[29] Paul's mission speech to Jews features the resurrection of Jesus "as the fulfilment of scriptural promises and the basis of forgiveness and justification,"[30] while the Gentile speeches seem very different because, while they introduce biblical concepts, they serve an audience that cannot be assumed to know the Bible or respect its authority.

Paul is the apostle to the Gentiles (Rom 11:13; Gal 2:8; 1 Tim 2:7), himself a Jew educated in Tarsus, which, with Athens

---

25. Blaiklock, "Areopagus Address," 190.

26. Dahle, "Acts 17:16–34," *Tyndale Bulletin*, 313, emphasis original.

27. See also Gray, "Implied Audiences," 212.

28. Legrand, "Areopagus Speech," 348; Dahle, "Acts 17:16–34," PhD diss., 17–18.

29. Downing, "Common Ground," 553, finds the Athens speech "is very similar to what we have already seen in Acts 14, but set at a slightly higher intellectual level."

30. Hansen, "Preaching and Defence of Paul," 295; cf. Green, *Evangelism in the Early Church*, 151–52.

and Alexandria, was a renowned "university city," and so he has a foot in both the Jewish and Greco-Roman worlds.[31] Luke's narrative world in Acts is broader than the near-monoculture of Israel. Acts 2:5–11 mentions some eighteen ethnicities or places of origin (though the audience is primarily Jews from those places). Acts 6 settles a dispute between Grecian and Hebraic Jews, while four other groups of Jews oppose the gospel (6:9). We meet an Ethiopian (ch. 8) and an Italian centurion (ch. 10). We see Gentiles receiving the word (ch. 11), and the church formally deciding what to do about the Gentile influx (ch. 15), "a watershed event in Luke's story-world."[32] Ethnicity is often described as important (e.g., 13:1; 16:1; 17:4), and Acts often describes travel to various places and cultural groups (e.g., 13:4–5; 16:6–9).

This interest in cultures is particularly true in the description of Athens, where Luke emphasizes the "pluralistic context of the *agora*."[33] In 17:17, Paul speaks to synagogue attenders, both Jews and Gentiles who are fellow travelers with Jewish monotheism. Then with an almost seamless transition, Paul, a citizen of both worlds, speaks daily in the agora with whoever chanced to be around: one can only imagine what variety of views existed in that cosmopolis. As well as ethnic origins, class no doubt played a role: we have already seen Paul hastily address "superstitious barbarians in Lystra" (Acts 14), and are about to witness a "reasoned address to sceptical philosophers in Athens."[34] Paul meets exponents of the two major schools of philosophy, which rivalled each other (another division). The response of the agora audience is also segmented: in 17:18, "some say" he is a nobody, while "others say" he is promoting foreign deities. We are told that the native Athenians and the *xenoi*, or foreigners, living there share at least one thing in common: a love for novelty (17:21). Similarly, Paul's speech does not assume "a monolithic Gentile audience but

---

31. Charles, "Engaging," 50.
32. Gray, "Implied Audiences," 207.
33. Dahle, "Acts 17 as an Apologetic Model," 2.
34. Hansen, "Preaching," 295.

## Asking Big Questions

rather engages multiple implied readers."[35] This audience further segments itself by three different responses: mocking, procrastination, and belief. (The story does not specify from which party Paul's adherents came.[36]) This is not the first time that apostolic preaching has divided an audience, and indeed resurrection has previously been the divisive issue (cf. Acts 23:6–10). Gray refers to "Luke's habit, seen in the gospel and Acts, of making distinctions between various groups and their response to his protagonists."[37] And so, as Charles also observes, there is "a remarkable amount of detail given in Luke's narrative" not only to "the content of Paul's speech" but also "the social context in which it is delivered."[38]

How much thought do contemporary evangelists give to audience research? Since the 1950s, advertising and marketing companies have employed some of the best psychology graduates in an effort to map the public mind and mood with the aim of selling people things—indeed, of creating appetites for things they do not really need or else, one assumes, they would buy them without advertising. The obvious materialism and exploitation inherent in this system have understandably deterred many evangelicals from wanting a part of it, and they have contented themselves with distant critique. Yet the market has always been a key site of human interaction and culture and for the exchange of ideas, and Paul was not too proud to work the agora, spending energy and effort on the range of people passing through. And it was his marketplace ministry that secured his invitation to the Areopagus, and provided the "context and background,"[39] and probably useful research and experience, for his work there.

Is the church generally following his example? Do we divide our time and resources between the "synagogue" and the agora, or do nonbelievers receive less of our resources, partly because

---

35. Gray, "Implied Audiences," 205.

36. Contra Hansen, "Preaching," 311, who claims Epicureans mocked Paul before and after, and Stoics were open to hearing more.

37. Gray, "Implied Audiences," 213.

38. Charles, "Engaging," 47.

39. Dahle, "Acts 17:16–34," PhD diss., 153.

they do not vote on church boards? What if those who seek to understand the market for purely commercial reasons are ahead of those of us who are trying to give the free gift of the gospel? What if in this sense the "children of darkness are in their generation wiser than the children of light" (Luke 16:8)? It seems obvious that evangelists and apologists should enlist the help of market research, and educate themselves enough to manage and understand it. Yet this suggestion is often resisted. The language of marketing can sound to some like "worldly business" rather than ministry. It can also sound exclusive. If we are targeting a certain demographic, does that mean we do not love or care for people outside it? Should we try to limit the type of fish caught in the gospel net? I have noticed church committees like it when you seem to have done your marketing homework, but that many seem uncomfortable that the implication of targeting a certain group of people means not particularly targeting another. For example, a committed youth pastor presents an outreach strategy for high school students, but someone on the committee objects that older people will not like the drums and guitars. Do older people not have souls to save? Do older people not pay for all this? And so the strategy can be watered down into a bland, grey sludge that tries to please everybody and ends up reaching only the faithful. Or start a ministry to university students which, as part of balanced pastoral care, addresses their intellectual questions, and someone can object that these meetings make some people feel stupid and confused, forgetting that a university meeting that reaches early high school students is probably not reaching its stated audience. I know of no research on this issue, but I have a sense that this may be why so much of evangelical preaching, both live and on TV, targets a "lowest common denominator" audience. This is an issue that the church needs to address.

Paul certainly tried for all demographics in Athens, but not at once: he responded appropriately to whoever was in front of him, whether in the synagogue (17:17), the marketplace (17:17-18) or the Areopagus (17:19-33)—and Luke makes no bones about using different methods to target different demographics.

Asking Big Questions

In a series of addresses and incidents Paul and others directly interacted with the ideas and concerns of a number of major social groups. As the narrative of Acts (and the history of the early church) makes clear, each of these groups came to be represented in the early church. The apologetic approaches illustrated in Acts led to conversions within each of these groups.[40]

This Apostolic example seems relevant and exemplary for the contemporary church.

## Epicureans: "Our Highest Good Is Pleasure"

One major segment of Paul's audience was Epicurean. This school of philosophy was found by Epicurus (340–270 BC), who came from an Athenian family living on the balmy island of Samos.[41] It taught that the highest human good was pleasure (*hedone*), a sense of tranquillity (*ataraxia*), and freedom from pain and disturbing passions and superstitions, especially the fear of death. Over Epicurus's garden was a sign: "Stranger, here you will do well to tarry; here our highest good is pleasure."[42] This view is materialism in the true sense. It sees the universe as the product of chance processes, with randomness at the base of all. And this leads to personal materialism.

This view has been extremely influential. It influenced thinkers behind the great experiment of the French Revolution. It influenced John Locke, and also Thomas Jefferson, who called himself an Epicurean,[43] and who wrote into the US Constitution the idea that "all men" have "inalienable rights such as life, liberty, and the pursuit of happiness." On the other side of politics, Karl Marx wrote his doctoral thesis on "The Difference between the Democritean and Epicurean Philosophy of Nature," and wrote extensively about

---

40. McGrath, "Biblical Models for Apologetics, Part 1," 10.
41. Blaiklock, "Areopagus Address," 181.
42. Seneca, Epistulae morales ad Lucilium, XXI.
43. Jefferson to William Short, 11 Oct. 1819, 136.

## Theological Background

Epicurus.[44] Epicurus was also influential on Artur Schopenhauer[45] and had "great significance" for Friedrich Nietzsche.[46]

Epicurus himself was not, as sometimes popularly portrayed, a wildly excessive hedonist. He would not have agreed with the famous punk slogan, "Live Fast, Die Young and Leave a Pretty Corpse." He was a long-term hedonist, who said that the wise person "curbed passion, scorned excess, lust, ambition, for all have aftermath of pain." He limited his desires so that disappointment and anxiety would be minimized, and looked for "health, quietness, simplicity," yet Epicureanism was "rapidly corrupted by those who sought a philosophical cloak for self-indulgence."[47]

Epicurus was an atomist. After Leucippus and Democritus, he argued that the universe is eternal, and that the random, unguided play of atoms mindlessly forms everything in the physical world, including people. Contemporary scientific materialism and the cultural nihilism that often accompanies it can be traced back to Greek atomists, especially Epicurus.[48] Revived in the early Renaissance, Epicureanism fed into "the modern reductionist, materialist framework for describing nature," fleshed out by Charles Darwin and Friedrich Nietzsche and Jean-Paul Sartre, even the nihilism of Woody Allen and *Seinfeld*.[49] While contemporary scientists would describe quarks and quasars and gluons, and critique the atomists for assuming that atoms are impenetrable, and that there are an infinite number of them,[50] Epicurus was an important influence on the thinking of pioneering chemist Robert Boyle (1627–1692),

---

44. Marx's thesis (written 1841; published 1902) is available at http://www.marxists.org/archive/marx/works/1841/dr-theses/index.htm; see also Marx's Notebooks on Epicurrean Philosophy, at http://www.marxists.org/archive/marx/works/1839/notebook.

45. See, e.g., Safranski, *Schopenhauer*, 106.

46. See Vincenzo, "Nietzsche and Epicurus," 383.

47. Blaiklock, "Areopagus Address," 182.

48. Wiker and Witt, *Meaningful World*, 15–16.

49. Ibid., 16–17.

50. Ibid., 120.

mediated through Pierre Gassendi (1592–1655),[51] and on the non-anthropocentric assumptions that governed astronomy.[52]

Epicureanism does have overlaps with Paul's message: that the divine is eternal and blessed; that everyone could find sufficient knowledge about the divine; that the divine does not live in man-made temples or need sacrifices or anything else from humans:[53] yet for Epicureans, the gods were not particularly interested in people, and so Paul's argument ends up in a critique of Epicureanism, because God is "not far" but immanent.[54]

Paul's notion of final judgment would have sounded strange. For Epicureans, death was the end.[55] Epicurus wrote, "Death is nothing to us; for the body, when it has been resolved into its elements, has no feeling and that which has no feelings is nothing to us."[56] Epicureans might write on their tombstones: *Non fui, fui, non sum, non curo* (I was not, I was, I am not, I do not care). Some contemporary humanists have adopted this: Bruce argues that paganism and atheism since have "never been able to devise anything appreciably better."[57] Certainly this view is common in contemporary atheist literature. For example, atheist broadcaster and filmmaker Phillip Adams writes, "I believe and have always believed that life is totally meaningless and we have no destiny, no purpose, no author. We just *are*. For a little while, anyway. Then we aren't."[58]

So it could be argued that secular people in Sydney are somewhat Epicurean, even if they may not know the full meaning of the term.

In their Christian apologetic response, Wiker and Witt deploy both scientific arguments and literary parallels to demonstrate the

51. Ibid., 127.
52. Ibid., 149–50.
53. Schnabel, "Contextualising Paul," 180.
54. Cf. Carson, *Gagging of God*, 202.
55. Hansen, "Preaching," 312.
56. Cited in Winter, "Introducing the Athenians to God," 50.
57. Bruce, *Book of Acts*, 331.
58. Adams, "OK, Adams," 157.

meaning that exists in nature, for example, the layers of language-like meaning in human DNA, and to demonstrate the barrenness of nihilism and reductionism for the view of the self. The *Big Questions* project will take a similar approach.

## Stoics: The Gods Are in All

The Stoic philosophical school was found by Zeno from Cyprus (340–265 BC), and took its name from Zeno's preferred place of teaching, the *stoa poikile*, or "painted colonnade," in the agora, which was right near where Paul likely taught in Athens. Stoicism encouraged people to be logical and prized self-sufficiency (*autarkeia*, cf. 2 Cor 9:8; 1 Tim 6:6), and to live in tune with nature. It saw the gods or God (Stoic writers used the terms almost interchangeably[59]) as one great world soul, and was thus pantheistic (or panentheistic[60]) rather than teaching a personal god. God ruled the world by providence, as proved from "the miracles of nature and from the gods' care for human beings."[61] Evil and suffering were not a disproof of God's sovereignty, because humans were free. The universe was "a living whole, filled and animated by one soul," and yet God's will was not always done: the Stoic taught that "God is indeed in all, save in the doings of bad men, for man is free."[62] This is a precursor of the "Christian Free Will Defense" developed more recently by Alvin Plantinga.[63]

The Stoics believed in the *cosmopolis*, or "world city in which all truly free souls had equal citizen rights, helped to break down national and class distinctions,"[64] a concept which Paul bridges to in speaking of one common ancestor of humanity (17:26). Stoicism encouraged high morals. For Zeno, being rich and com-

---

59. Winter, "Introducing the Athenians to God," 49–53.
60. Dahle, "Acts 17:16–34," PhD diss., 64.
61. Schnabel, "Contextualising Paul," 180.
62. Blaiklock, "Areopagus Address," 184.
63. See Plantinga, *God, Freedom, and Evil*.
64. Blaiklock, "Areopagus Address," 183–84.

fortable may be one thing, but history praises "goodness, virtue, heroism," and a person who cultivates goodness, even if they lose all else, cannot lose their character and so need not worry.[65] Stoics sought a "good death," and could see certain suicides as ethical and noble. Stoicism also taught a concept of final judgment by God,[66] which would have common ground with Paul's statement about coming judgment (17:31), though Paul says that the judgment is by "a man chosen by God."

Even Paul's method may owe something to Stoicism. He taught the attributes of the unknown God, and Stoics would often argue in this style. Cicero, in *De natura deorum*, says they "first prove that the gods exist; next they explain their nature; then they show that the world is governed by them; and lastly, they care for the fortunes of mankind."[67] Thus Paul's speech "may have consciously followed sections of the standard presentation of the nature of divinity used by the Stoics."[68]

Yet his argument eventually counters Stoic pan(en)theism, since it positions God as the Creator and Sovereign of history.[69]

## Some New Thing from "the Sparrow"

Paul is called a *spermologos* (17:18), a "seed-picker," "gutter sparrow," someone who picked up scraps of learning in the market. The apostle, a spiritual and intellectual champion to Christians, is seen as contemptible, intellectually and socially, and a mere plagiarist from real thinkers.[70] This contempt is nothing new for prophets and other messengers, and even for Christ himself, and it feels strangely familiar to contemporary Christian speakers. When some New Atheists call themselves "Brights"[71] and

65. Ibid.
66. Winter, "Introducing the Athenians to God," 49–53.
67. Cicero, *De natura deorum* II.4, quoted in Hansen, "Preaching," 312.
68. Winter, "Introducing the Athenians to God," 49.
69. Carson, *Gagging of God*, 202.
70. Hansen, "Preaching," 311.
71. Hitchens, *God Is Not Great*, 5, takes Dawkins and Dennett to task for

## Theological Background

Christians "faith-heads," suggesting we are intellectually inferior, the same slur is repeated, often as an attempt to shut the Christian out of public debate. Yet the fact that Paul was later invited to the Areopagus suggests that he was at least respected for his learning and logic, and provides a strategic staircase for contemporary Christians to be invited into the marketplace of today. We need to teach in the "synagogue" with those who believe the Bible, but also get out into the marketplace so as to interact with whoever comes past and whatever new theories are around. While the malls and shopping precincts of contemporary cities are marketplaces, there is now the virtual marketplace of the media, a gigantic public space which is truly global in scope. Evangelicals often perceive it as difficult to access this—and perhaps it is partly true because of prejudice, but partly also because we have not even tried.

A contemporary communicator also feels connection to the ephemerality of Athenian culture, where novelty is prized (17:21), yesterday's hero is "so five minutes ago" and eclipsed by the Next Big Thing, and the only constant is change. For Blaiklock, this is decadence. Luke, "often the master of brief irony," notes the "shallow artificiality" of people who spend all their time on novelty, of "glib talk for the sake of talking," of "the commercialisation of knowledge and culture, the horde who lived by wits and words, in short, all the sham, the artificiality, the dishonesty, and empty pride of a city living on its past."[72] Cultural critics like Neil Postman[73] have pointed out similar trends in the contemporary culture, particularly in relation to television, with its quick changes of thought lessening attention spans and producing passive consumers. This is even more true of the Internet, where the user controls the transitions and the next subject is only a hypertext click away. Just before Athens, the demographic Paul encountered were the text-reading, critical-thinking Bereans, who "received the message with great eagerness, and searched the Scriptures daily" (17:11).

---

this "cringe-making proposal."

72. Blaiklock, "Areopagus Address," 177–79.
73. Postman, *Amusing Ourselves to Death*.

## Asking Big Questions

In striking contrast,[74] the Athenians, while priding themselves on living in the home of philosophy, actually seem shallow, which sets up narratively for Paul's message about culpable ignorance. And yet Paul seems determined to work graciously with their condition—*dielegeto*, discussing, debating, addressing, reasoning—and to stimulate their reason as a step toward faith, working from the known to the unknown.

It seems that the contemporary evangelist needs the skills of a publicist in linking the timeless Christian message to whatever is currently getting exposure, and popularizing it into key messages. For example, I co-wrote a popular book and website in response to the media juggernaut of *The Da Vinci Code*, which was undermining people's faith in the accuracy of the story of Jesus. After Dan Brown's bestselling novel, amid heavy publicity about the release of the first film, our website (www.thedavincidecode.com) peaked at 112 thousand hits per month from six continents in May 2006. Previous months had been almost as high. Then the film launched and, by August, we were averaging only eleven thousand hits per month. By our measure, interest had dropped around 90 percent in three months. Our explanation was that the film was critically and popularly panned, and did not rate like the novel. We now average some four thousand hits per month, which is still worthwhile (especially as little effort is required to maintain a web page) but illustrates the long tail of public interest. Responding to cultural trends this can be difficult for churches, and I admit that I wish we had started the Da Vinci project a year or more earlier, or when I first read the book and guessed it would be a bestseller. It can be difficult for churches to develop an entrepreneurial culture of rapid response, standing ready to release writers from other responsibilities and having project funding held on standby and management structures that can respond quickly and efficiently, of course with sufficient critical consultation, and distribution systems on standby. We need contemporary sons of Issachar, who understand the times and know what God's people need to do (1 Chron 12:32). Paul, as an independent, self-supporting minister,

---

74. Winter, "On Introducing Gods to Athens," 86.

was able to adapt quickly, but then his learning from his childhood onwards had prepared him for this. He was able to exploit his novelty value, and to leverage public criticism into an invitation to present in elite circles. As the old adage has it, "All publicity is good publicity." Often it seems that the Western media positions Christianity as the boring, predictable religion and other brands such as the Dalai Lama or Wicca can seem novel and exciting. Perhaps we need to develop the art of being controversial and interesting and drawing headlines. Paul managed to do this.

## Athenian and Biblical Communication

By Paul's day, Athens had long since lost the political power it held during the Golden Age, but it still had time-honored prestige and cultural leadership. Luke's brief narrative gives a real sense of Athens down to the details: the "argumentative character of the Athenians, the philosophers, the "unknown gods," the local slang" term *spermologos*[75]—all of these capture Athens[76] like a yellow cab and a cream cheese bagel suggest New York. Further, Luke portrays Paul's speaking style in the tradition of Socrates: he dialogues in the agora with all comers, he is charged with heralding foreign divinities, and he is put on trial for his new teaching.[77]

Paul uses an Athenian story about the unknown god to make known his God. Plato "preserves a tradition that Epimenides, the Cretan religious teacher and miracle-worker" was in Athens in 500 or 600 BC ("but dates are neither here nor there in a half-legendary situation"). "The story was that, to combat an epidemic, Epimenides directed the Athenians to loose sheep from the Areopagus, and wherever they lay down to build an altar 'to the unknown god' of the place, and to make sacrifice. Perhaps the story is an aetiological myth,"[78] yet it functions as part of Paul's argument:

75. Hemer, "Speeches of Acts," 242.

76. See Dahle, "Acts 17:16–34," PhD diss., 42.

77. Hansen, "Preaching," 310. Socrates also mounts philosophical critiques of religion, in his case polytheistic mythical religions.

78. Blaiklock, "Areopagus Address," 186.

he is not introducing new deities, but explicating the ancient God. Paul also quotes poets who were authoritative to his hearers. The words about living and moving and having our being in God come from Epimenides the Cretan. The line about us being the offspring of God comes from Aratus (b. 310 BC in Cilicia, Paul's own area), and it applies to Zeus,[79] so Paul is hardly endorsing all it says: these are "points of contact with the hearers, and illustrate the argument in terms familiar to them, but they in no way commit the speaker to acquiescence in their philosophical presuppositions."[80] And by the end of his speech, it becomes apparent that this is not mere flattery of superior culture. Paul encourages them that God cares for all nations, but does not suggest their religious art or architecture have brought them any closer to God;[81] rather he emphasizes that God has come close and we need to grope around and reach out for him. Yet this is humbling: it is blind people who grope. The blinded Cyclops gropes for the entrance to his cave in *Odyssey* 9.416, described with the same verb.[82] And how can humans, even the most cultured ones, boast if God is drawing so near and they are still groping?[83] They are wrong about idols representing God, wrong to think God inhabits their temples or needs them, and wrong to think polytheistically of each nation having its god. Yet this does not condemn natural theology[84] per se, only *their* theology. Their ignorance is culpable. It is treated gently at first— "whom you worship unknowingly"—but ignorance eventually requires repentance. (Culpable ignorance seems to be a theme in Luke: 9:44–45; 23:34; 3:17; 7:48–50.) It is "not simply a case of being epistemologically in the wrong place at the wrong time," but *agnountes* may well be "a lapse from God,"[85] requiring repentance (17:30). By the end of the speech one is tempted to reread Paul's

---

79. For the text, see Bruce, *Book of Acts*, 338–39.
80. Bruce, *Book of Acts*, 342.
81. Similarly Hansen, "Preaching," 316.
82. Blaiklock, "Areopagus Address," 188.
83. Marshall, *Acts of the Apostles*, 288.
84. Contra Hansen, "Preaching," 316.
85. Gray, "Implied Audiences," 214.

## Theological Background

opening line. He called his audience *deisidaimonesteros*, which can mean religious or "superstitious" (KJV). Polite challenge is clearly intended to their religious devotions and the views and paradigms supporting them.

For all his enculturation and seeking of common ground, Paul's content is solidly biblical. Some scholars have missed his frequent biblical allusions and assumed Paul's speech is purely Hellenistic, perhaps with a slight Christian add-on,[86] but these scriptural intertexts are part of Luke presenting this as a "prophetic speech" in continuity with prophets of the past.[87] Even Paul's initial reaction to idolatry is described with a word used in the Septuagint of God's response to idolatry (*paruxunein* 17:16, cf. Deut 32:16, 21; also Hos 8:5).

Paul's speech is rich with allusions to the Hebrew Bible. He says God created the world and everything in it (17:24; cf. Gen 1:1; Exod 20:11; Isa 42:5; and many others). No human building can contain God (17:24; cf. 1 Kgs 8:27; Isa 40:18–19; 42:6; 44:9–20; 45:15–24; 46:5–8; 66:1–2;[88] Job 32:8; and also Stephen's speech in Acts 7:48), though Euripides also said this.[89] God is not dependent on sacrifice (17:25; cf. Ps 50:9–12; cf. Mic 6:6–8). God gives life and breath and everything else (17:25; cf. Gen 2:7; Isa 42:5; Neh 9:6) and made all people from one man (17:26; cf. Gen 1:27–28) and ordained their territories (17:26; cf. Gen 10; Deut 32:8; Dan 2:21ff.; 4:37; 7:12, 15; Amos 9:7) so that people would reach out for him and find him (17:27; cf. Isa 45:19; Ps 14:2), though God is not far from each of us (17:27; cf. Ps 139:7–10), and we are his offspring (17:28; cf. Gen 1:26), so we should not view God as like human images (17:29; cf. Ps 115:4; 135:15; Isa 40:18–19). God will "judge the world in

---

86. See Dibelius, *Studies*, 67.

87. Litwak, "Israel's Prophets," 199. Dahle, "Acts 17:16–34," PhD diss., 66–68, lists intertexts in Scripture, and Jewish and Hellenistic literature. Carson, *Gagging God*, 313.

88. Pao, *Acts and the Isaianic New Exodus*, 193–208.

89. Bruce, *Book of Acts*, 336, cites fragment 968: "What house built by craftsmen could enclose the form divine within enfolding walls?"

righteousness," which is "another biblical expression"[90] (17:31; cf. Ps 9:8–9; 96:13; 98:9; and see also Rom 2:5, 16; 1 Cor 1:8; Phil 1:6, 10; 1 Thess 5:2, 4; 2 Thess 1:10; 2:2). God will judge by a man (17:31; cf. the "one like the son of man" in Dan 7:13, and Jesus' appropriation of this term, John 5:27). Dahle also suggests that Paul borrows the overall approach of "key OT apologists,"[91] particularly on idolatry. Paul also describes the "unknown god" in a way that suggests pagans do not really know much about God (cf. Isa 45:15).

Some scholars have wondered how much this speech is compatible with Paul's other teaching, yet his gospel always starts with knowing the true God by his works in creation and his revelation in human history (cf. Rom 1:18–32; 2:14–16; ).[92] Paul's comments to the Thessalonians suggest a similar topic outline was used in evangelistic work among them: conversion from idols to the living God, divine judgment to come, and the resurrection of Jesus (1 Thess 1:9–10), which seems to be Paul's standard "missionary process."[93] Quoting extra-biblical sources is also hardly without precedent in the Bible (cf. Luke 11:49; 1 Cor 6:12–13; 7:1; 15:33; Titus 1:12; 2 Pet 2:22; Jude 14).[94]

Some have suggested this speech is not Christological.[95] Yet perhaps "Paul avoided mentioning the name of Jesus, perhaps because he wanted to avoid the impression that he proclaimed 'foreign divinities' (17:18)."[96] One can hardly imagine Paul giving a gospel speech without mentioning the cross, and yet it is not explicitly mentioned at the Areopagus. Some have suggested he was simply interrupted before he could get to the cross, and was dismissed: "we will hear you again on this matter"[97]—yet

---

90. Bruce, *Book of Acts*, 340.
91. Dahle, "Acts 17:16–34," PhD diss., 164.
92. Ibid., 22.
93. See Dahle, "Acts 17:16–34," PhD diss., 46–47.
94. Ibid., 22n70.
95. E.g., Porter, *Paul of Acts*, 124.
96. Schnabel, "Contextualising Paul," 183.
97. Compare Horsley, "Speeches and Dialogue," 610, who sees interruption commonly used in Acts.

## Theological Background

this speech seems rhetorically complete.⁹⁸ The narrator certainly describes him as preaching the gospel publicly and habitually in Athens (εὐηγγελίζετο 17:18) and Paul uses similar terms (καταγγέλλω 17:23), as do his questioners (καταγγελεὺς 17:18). It seems apparent that his Areopagus speech is a follow-up to that explicit preaching of the cross, which confirms key aspects of the Christian worldview to those who may not have understood or who may have misunderstood. Hemer suggests that Paul could hardly "indulge Christological refinements which would be meaningless to a pagan audience, if they did not actually suggest a false picture."⁹⁹ Dahle argues that

> a pre-evangelistic presentation—on the nature of God, the human responsibility and the possibility and necessity of conversion—usually seems to be needed, if the deeper theological redemptive message of the cross is to be grasped by pagans who are biblically illiterate... The intention...was thus to present the Athenians with a Christian view of the world... so they could make sense of the Christian gospel (including the redemptive message of the cross of Christ) within a proper biblical framework.¹⁰⁰

Schnabel adds:

> Further, the overall shape of the speech is perfectly consistent with the gospel. It concludes with the idea that "people who approach God, the one true God, also approach Jesus, or must go through Jesus."¹⁰¹

As Bruce has written, "The speech as it stands admirably summarizes an introductory lesson in Christianity for cultured pagans...The essential content of the speech is biblical, but the presentation is Hellenistic."¹⁰²

---

98. Dahle, "Acts 17:16–34," PhD diss., 168–69.
99. Hemer, "Speeches of Acts," 254.
100. Dahle, "Acts 17:16–34," PhD diss., 169.
101. Schnabel, "Contextualising Paul," 185.
102. Bruce, *Book of Acts*, 341.

## Asking Big Questions

This serves as a challenge to contemporary gospel communicators. If excellent apologetic practice builds on-ramps to biblical revelation which connect with the street the listeners live on. Generally speaking, churches and individuals are better at one end of this than the other. Some preachers perform superb exegesis which never gets past AD 100, perhaps because they want to preach biblically rather than using their own pastoral nous to apply the message, a move which contains subjective judgments. This is biblical preaching but often does not connect. Others are so comfortable analyzing the culture that they almost seem to let the culture rewrite some biblical commandments and principles, and so do not challenge culture. Yet the Bible itself is constantly connecting timeless truths to people's present reality, and a good teacher relates "things new and old" (Matt 13:52). This is a model to aim for.

## Words about Images (Graven and Otherwise)

To his great credit, Paul, the "Hebrew of the Hebrews" (Phil 3:5), really *sees* this pagan city and its idols (17:16). He was very likely raised on the view that images were for weak-minded pagans. Today's tourist, climbing up from Dionysius the Areopagite Street to Mars Hill, where the *Areopagitica* is written in bronze, and boggling weak-kneed at the impossible beauty and perfect lines of the Parthenon, finds it difficult to get a sense of all this classic art being so opposed to the gospel.

> The modern visitor who...sees the breath-taking majesty of the shattered Parthenon, mellow in its golden marble, superbly placed, has no thought of Athene, who once stood in the dim interior, the object of man's devotion. He may trace the base of another colossal image of Athens' patron goddess in the precinct. It stood with spear upraised so high that sailors off Sunion caught the sun's glint on its point from forty miles away. When the blond Goths intruded at the beginning of the dark fifth century

after Christ, they scattered in wild fright at the first sight of the image…The reverence of the Athenian, the terror of the Goth, the repugnance of the Jew for blasphemy in bronze and stone, mean nothing to him…

Perhaps the Christian can still touch the edge of that deep sensation only in the revolting presence of the phallic image. Some fragments, vast and intricately carved on Delos, reveal the gross mingling of carnality and religion which stirred the wrath of the Hebrew prophets.[103]

The violence and pornography of these myths, the ugly false gods and systems of thought which they made beautiful, and the damnable lies they immortalised in stone, would have been part of what so upset Paul.[104]

We can get some sense of the cultural issues in play from a more recent debate between two cultural critics, Neil Postman, a conservative humanist, and Camille Paglia, who calls herself a lapsed Catholic and neo-pagan. Postman argues: "The image is so seductive."[105] He points out that two of the Bible's first three commandments "concern communications: the prohibition against making graven images and taking the Lord's name in vain." In marketing terms, this is protecting God's branding by refusing to cheapen it with a logo or let his brand-name be misused, so it constitutes visual and verbal protection of God's brand. Postman says:

> Moses chose writing…to conceptualize this nonvisual, nonmaterial God. Writing is the perfect medium because, unlike pictures or oral tradition, the written word is a symbol system *of* a symbol system, twice removed from the reality and perfect for describing a…non-physical, abstracted divinity. Moses smartly chose the right communication strategy. Moses was the first person who ever said, more or less, "Don't watch TV; go do your homework."[106]

---

103. Blaiklock, "Areopagus Address," 176–77.
104. Cf. Parente, "St. Paul's Address," 144.
105. Postman, *Amusing Ourselves to Death*, 46.
106. Postman, *Amusing Ourselves to Death*, 45.

## Asking Big Questions

By contrast, Paglia is much more positive about images. She argues with the beginning of the Gospel of John, which claims that in the beginning was the Word:

> But John got it all wrong. "In the beginning was nature." That's the first sentence in my book. Nature—violent, chaotic, unpredictable, uncontrollable—predates and stands in opposition to the ordered, structured world created by the word, by the law, by the book-centred culture of Judeo-Christianity. The image—which is pagan and expressive of nature's sex and violence—was outlawed by Moses in favour of the word.[107]

Since then, different branches of Christianity have been shaped around their chosen media. Postman again:

> Luther called the printing press the "supremest act of grace by which the Gospel can be driven forward." And it was. As a result of Luther's reformation, the intellectual geography of Europe flipped. Until then Venice, in the South of Europe, was the leading printing centre and one of Europe's intellectual capitals. Then the Catholic Church got nervous about it, because of the possibility of further heresy, and began to restrict the printing press... England, Scandinavia, Germany became the realm of the word, and the south returned to spectacle. Catholicism resorted increasingly to ornament and beautiful music and painting...The North, the home of the austere Protestant, concentrated on the word, until it found its greatest fulfilment here in the first political system built on the word alone.[108]

Paglia counters, "My first childhood memories are of images, fantastic images, created by the Catholic church...like Bernini's St. Theresa having a spiritual orgasm" and "St. Sebastian, nude, arrows piercing his flesh, red blood dripping down...Here were spectacular pagan images standing right next to the altar." She argues that the music and videos of Madonna (the US artist, not the

---

107. Postman and Paglia, "She Wants Her TV," 45.
108. Ibid., 46.

## Theological Background

religious figure) are "revealing the eroticism and sadomasochism, the pagan ritualism and idolatry in Italian Catholicism."[109] Paglia associates the word with the Apollonian principle, and the image with the Dionysian. She argues that the "history of Western civilisation has been a constant struggle between these two impulses, an unending tennis match between cold Apollonian categorisation and Dionysian lust and chaos." And what is the ideal? "Ancient Greco-Roman culture harnessed the dynamic duality" of both.[110]

This is the culture in which Paul operated. He could hardly carve competing images, but he analyzed the images using words. (I note in passing that the cross-media challenge of this is immense. As the old saying goes, "Talking about art is like dancing about architecture.") Paul, the Jewish intellectual and wordsmith, analyzes pagan image culture, even though he personally finds it emotionally upsetting. He knows that "what pagans sacrifice, they offer to demons and not to God" (1 Cor 10:20).[111] And yet he does not break off his contact with the culture and withdraw from "the world," as some Christian fundamentalists have sought to do. Nor does he unleash a shrill tirade, but he allows his deep feeling to motivate a well-reasoned and well-targeted strategy of gentle persuasion, using their images as a starting point. This is a gracious and redemptive use of culture.

And today? For Postman, "Luther would join Moses in saying that the cult of the word is defenceless in the face of the image."[112] In considering the question of how religion can use television, Postman points out dangers of televisual culture: it does not require (much) critical thinking, comprehension or even focused attention. It can trivialize a culture, reducing political debate to short sound bites and entertainment, with brief image projections of the candidates rather than sustained analysis. For Postman, the attempt to screen religion is fraught with danger of reducing sacred mysteries to mere entertainment, compared to other entertain-

109. Ibid.
110. Ibid., 48.
111. Bruce, *Book of Acts*, 329.
112. Postman and Paglia, "She Wants Her TV," 54.

ments with which they are in competition for viewer attention. He argues that Jesus would probably refuse to go onto a talk show.[113]

Yet Paul went into the agora. This was entering the popular culture, the marketplace. His speaking would have been subject to competition from jugglers, philosophers, magicians and the man selling statues of Athena—any of these could have been more entertaining than he was, but it was better to compete in that market than to wait in a temple or synagogue for people to come to him. Christian communicators have a choice today, but it is much better to enter the market, even if some call you a *spermologos*, than to make no effort at all.

Today we have another option. Our age is often viewed as the age of the image. Visual media are everywhere, not just dominating the market place but having become the marketplace themselves. Images advertise, educate, influence political debate and entertain. (Interestingly, Jews have become some of the greatest image-makers, and a quick scan for Jewish names in the credits of many films shows the cinema is almost as Jewish an institution as the synagogue.) Many churches have maintained a critical stance to film and television. Influenced by the "culture wars" of the United States, it has not been uncommon for conservative evangelicals to see cinema as "Satan's church,"[114] and to critique it from without. But more recently, some evangelicals are beginning to reengage. For example, Crouch argues that it is not enough to critique, copy, or consume culture. Christians ought to be making it.[115]

A Christian filmmaker can hardly stay aloof from the culture of images, but must enter it, understand its rules and compete in it. They may choose not to use pagan images of gratuitous violence and pornography, but they can make the images they want to tell stories and to argue for their faith.

Film of course is not only about images. It also requires beautiful words. Dramatist Patsy Rodenburg writes:

---

113. Postman, *Entertaining*.
114. Cf. Kent, "Pop Culture," 52.
115. Crouch, *Culture Making*.

*Theological Background*

> Most of us, I think, no longer trust in words. We have forgotten and, in some instances, have lost forever language's ancient mesmerising power...Somewhere along the line we stopped being an oral society...Storytelling, discussion, debate or just the simple enjoyment of words and word games ceased to be part of our daily lives... We have grown accustomed to thinking that government and media of every sort have done a great deal to corrupt the need for honest and accurate words in our lives... We live in an age of "sound bites" where even our leading politicians can only speak in disconnected fragments and simplistic homilies. The "great speech" is no longer in them.[116]

A strong film, Christian or otherwise, can exemplify Paglia's "dynamic duality" of images and words together.

## Paul's Themes Today

It seems safe to assume that Paul's message to the Athenian audience would contain key features of apostolic Christianity, and that these should provide the agenda for Christian apologetic witness today. These themes include "biblical doctrines of creation, God, man, and the resurrection."[117]

Paul clearly leads with creation (17:24).[118] To establish this foundational idea, "a common apologetic bridge to the pagan mind is employed: nature itself."[119] This is used to reveal God's general revelation. Demarest observes that general revelation

> affords all people of all times and places rudimentary knowledge of God as Creator and moral law-giver. It also affords the Christian evangelist significant points of contact with the non-Christian world, thereby serving as a valuable pre-evangelistic tool. General revelation,

---

116. Rodenburg, *Need for Words*, 4–5.
117. Charles, "Engaging," 55.
118. Ibid., 54.
119. Ibid., 56.

however, does not yield that higher knowledge of God that is redemptive.[120]

Paul's speech refers to general revelation at first but moves into special revelation.[121] Indeed, the Bible often confronts a pagan view which interprets nature as chaotic (see Ps 73:12–14; 88:9–11; Job 38:8–11; Prov 8:28–29; Jer 5:22; 31:35; 38:36).[122]

Creation is always basic to Paul's theology. In Romans, natural theology is used to show that all people, even those Gentiles without the law, are "without excuse" (Rom 1:20), and his Athens speech, while expressed more tactfully and positively, eventually reaches the same conclusion.[123]

So creation must be crucial to the gospel. Since Darwin, Christianity is divided on questions of creation. Fundamentally, did God simply set up initial constants and conditions and allow things to evolve, or did God perform design creation? If the latter, was it relatively recent or ancient, and how long did God take to do it? This is not the place to debate these questions, but to recognize that some doctrine of creation is fundamental to the gospel. Simply put, if I am merely a hominid with a larger frontal lobe and less body hair, why should I not act that way? Why should I not feed, fight and fornicate my genes into the next generation? To have any sense of sin, I would have to have sufficient intellectual basis for a moral law beyond survival of the fittest, encouraging love of neighbour. This is a problem that has vexed atheistic moral philosophers.[124] Biblical natural theology soon points to human moral accountability (cf. Rom 2:14 or the three movements of Ps 19), but what other ultimate basis for it can be found? Hence the classic "moral argument" for God's existence, which we plan to use in our film series.

---

120. Demarest, "General and Special Revelation," 151, and Demarest, *General Revelation*, 227–62.

121. Cf. Dahle, "Acts 17:16–34," PhD diss., 175.

122. See Charles, "Engaging," 56n52.

123. For examples, see Hemer, "Speeches of Acts," 251.

124. There is a vast bibliography on this point, as will be discussed briefly in the Moral Argument section of chap. 4.

## Theological Background

Further, Paul claims that God's redemptive purposes can be seen in history. This is the Bible's overall claim in writing "theological history" of Israel and its interactions with surrounding nations. This connects with the claim that history is moving to some goal, some end-point, and that this will involve judgment. The alternative today is the Enlightenment view whereby history is explained in terms of psychology, economics, class struggle or other theories, but never by a divine hand.

Human anthropology is also crucial: we are God's children, but what does that mean? Here creation is crucial. In what sense can a person be spiritual in a merely material universe? What can the soul be, other than a quaint religious expression emptied of real meaning? And what is resurrection? Clearly, "*creation ex nihilo* and bodily resurrection" are "inextricably related" concepts. Both were "untenable to the Hellenistic mindset, due to contemporary views of the universe, the body, and the soul."[125] Indeed the Areopagus was founded on the view that "when a man dies, the earth drinks up his blood. There is no resurrection (*anastasis*)."[126] And so Paul's comments on creation are seen as an overture to his gospel presentation on resurrection, the topic which proved so unpalatable to many of his hearers, and which broke up the meeting. Most Greek thinking saw the soul as living on in the underworld, or reincarnation, or living on another Platonic plane. Stoics thought it may be reabsorbed back into God, a theory not dissimilar to contemporary reincarnation. Epicureans thought the soul had only a material basis, and so died with the body, which is similar to materialists today. None of these worldviews had space for the "standing up" or resurrection of the body.[127] These issues still generate huge interest today. Who am I? Am I more than merely physical? This is the approach for one of our film episodes.

The resurrection claim also brings with it a lot of freight. It suggests this "man" has ultimate authority in the judgment. It

---

125. Charles, "Engaging," 54.

126. Winter, "Introducing the Athenians to God," 47, citing Aeschylus, *Eumenides*, 647–48.

127. Bruce, *Book of Acts*, 343; Hemer, "Speeches of Acts," 244.

invites curiosity and further investigation into Jesus, including seeking historical evidence for the resurrection.[128] It is disturbing because it threatens cozy relativism and universalist notions of afterlife, and motivates specific enquiry and true repentance.[129] This is still the case today. Blaiklock describes

> those today who profess a search for an elusive God, greater and higher than "the God of revelation," and who end bewildered with something not unlike the Stoic "phusis," some ancient pantheism dressed in modern words, an impersonal and scarcely personal Force, created in the image of Tillich, Bultmann, and the Bishop of Woolwich.[130]

C. S. Lewis's analysis of this issue is worth quoting at length:

> We who defend Christianity find ourselves constantly opposed not by the irreligion of our hearers, but by their real religion. Speak about beauty, truth, and goodness, or about a God who is simply the indwelling principle of these three, speak about a great spiritual force pervading all things, a common mind of which we are all parts, a pool of generalized spirituality to which we can all flow, and you will command friendly interest. But the temperature drops as soon as you mention a God who has purposes and performs particular actions, who does one thing and not another, a concrete, choosing, commanding, prohibiting God with a determinate character. People become embarrassed and angry.[131]

> An impersonal God—well and good. A subjective God of beauty, truth and goodness, inside our own heads—better still. A formless life force surging through us, a vast power which we can tap—best of all. But God Himself, alive, pulling at the other end of the cord... that is quite another matter...There comes a moment when people

---

128. Dahle, "Acts 17:16–34," PhD diss., 193.
129. Cf. Charles, "Engaging," 61.
130. Blaiklock, "Areopagus Address," 188.
131. Lewis, *Miracles*, 130.

*Theological Background*

who have been dabbling in religion ("Man's search for God"!) suddenly draw back. Supposing we really found Him?...Worse still, supposing He had found us? So it is a sort of Rubicon. One goes across; or not.[132]

This was the challenge faced by Paul. It is still a major challenge in telling the gospel today. I have found this often in live presentations, and am trying to apply that experience in the three film episodes we will do about Jesus. I have a sense that we will strike this problem from episode 10, when we introduce an Old Testament messianic prediction.

Simply put, the *Big Questions* series aims to communicate what is in principle the same message two millennia later, allowing apostolic Christianity as preached by Paul to shape its topic outline.

## Paul's Strategy Today

Dahle sees Paul's key aims as being "to interest," "to persuade," and "to confront," showing an awareness of the presuppositions of the audience.[133] These are surely still relevant today for a target audience which, like Paul's, is biblically illiterate and pluralistic. The first rule for a filmmaker is to be interesting: without that, nothing else matters.

Of course there are cultural differences. Paul's audience were pre-Christian and pre-modern, while ours is post-Christian and postmodern (or, I would argue, post-postmodern). If postmoderns distrust *logos* and emphasize *pathos*,[134] then logic must be used humbly and movingly, with awareness of deconstruction. The Pauline argument of human obligation to God's authority must be justified against "postmodern suspicions" and the "consumerism" which would make the individual the center of the world, and if Christ's resurrection is to be "seen as resonating with ultimate hu-

---

132. Ibid., 150.
133. Dahle, "Acts 17:16–34," *Tyndale Bulletin*, 314.
134. Dahle, "Acts 17:16–34," PhD diss., 259.

man concerns," it must justified against postmodern ambiguity and suspicion about history.¹³⁵ McGrath suggests that access points may be a "sense of longing" for meaning and purpose and fulfilment in life,¹³⁶ and that the apologist should look for "signals of transcendence"¹³⁷ that are meaningful to postmodern people.

As will be explained in the next chapter, our target demographic is more educated than average and so may not be exclusively postmodern in outlook. One notes that the New Atheists are largely modernist in their worldview, and their influence on this demographic is strong. If science and logic are trusted, then this is the domain in which a large part of our apologetic work will be done.

The technique of

> connecting with the hearers, correcting their misconceptions, conversing with their theological or ideological framework, convicting them of the compromises with their own consciences in the light of their intellectual commitment are critical steps. It is also necessary to confront them with their need of repentance toward God and faith in the Lord Jesus Christ because of the coming day of judgement. These are all essential features of an apologetic that is distinctly Christian and biblical.¹³⁸

## The Electronic Agora

Today the main marketplace is virtual and electronic.

Dalton has argued that, just as Paul engaged the content of Athenian culture and used its cultural forms of discourse well, so the contemporary church should use electronic media because these "are the marketplace and Areopagus of the day."¹³⁹ More

---

135. Dahle, "Acts 17:16–34," *Tyndale Bulletin*, 316.
136. McGrath, *Unknown God*, 7–71.
137. McGrath, *Bridge-Building*, 188, cites Berger, *Rumour of Angel*, 61–94.
138. Winter, "Introducing the Athenians to God," 58.
139. Dalton, "Electronic Areopagus," 33.

## Theological Background

precisely, one could say that the mass media are the electronic agora and niche media (not to say elite media) are the electronic Areopagus.

Dahle, noting the observation that the Athenian agora was "the first mass medium in history"[140] (or at least one of the first: Jericho likely had a market square), raises the question "whether, and in that case to what extent, a given communicative context—such as the contemporary media—affects the shape and influence of argumentative strategies in apologetics." He argues that media should be carefully analyzed to determine how they function as a communicative context for apologetics. He argues this analysis should

> address various significant roles of the media in relation to apologetics—e.g., as a formative cultural presence (media as "wallpaper"), as an arena (media as "marketplace of ideas"), and as a story-teller (media as "secular pulpit")—as well as the extent to which the content, the approach, the arguments and the aims of the Acts 17 model are relevant in a communicative context of "postmodern media."[141]

Dahle summarizes recent Christian critiques.[142] He finds

> Elaine Storkey mentions some underlying perspectives or ideologies, which, consciously or unconsciously, direct much of the change: "individualism," "economism," "scientism," "relativism" and "search for meaning." These ideologies constitute the heart of modern idolatry.[143]

These contemporary idols must be analyzed carefully. The apologist today must convince the individualist that there are benefits in belonging and giving; demonstrate to the economically-driven person that there is a high cost to materialism, and greater

---

140. For this quote he credits Berg Eriksen, *Budbringerens overtak: perspektiver på skriftkulturen* (Oslo: Universitetsforlaget, 1987).
141. Dahle, "Acts 17:16–34," PhD diss., 281.
142. Dahle, "Apologetic Approach to the Media," 2.3.2.
143. Ibid., citing Storkey, "Change and Decay," 114–23.

## Asking Big Questions

satisfactions in love and grace and relationship; to the scientifically-driven person that science and faith can coexist quite happily and tensions can be creative, but also that there are more things in heaven and earth than can be dreamt of by science; and to the relativist that some things are absolutely true; and that meaning can be discovered along the way.

Dahle also notes the rival ideologies noted by Os Guinness:

> 1) General secularism (liberal humanism and Marxism), 2) general syncretism (New Age, mysticism, and local, national or religious syncretism), and 3) traditional religious alternatives stressing transcendence and totality (Christianity, Judaism and Islam). Common to both secularism and syncretism is "the implicit relativism in their truth claims and the evolutionary optimism in their view of history."[144]

It will be important to find out which of these are most influential on our selected target audience, and to address their presuppositions.

Dahle argues that such pluralism may lead many media consumers to a "relativistic view of truth, religion and morality." Yet he nuances this with a comment from Lesslie Newbigin, who argues that

> the principle of pluralism only applies to the private world of "beliefs and values," whereas in the public world of "facts" no heretics are allowed. The dichotomy between the private and the public world is the operating plausibility structure of the modern, secular world.[145]

Thus it will be important to speak to people's private intuitions and beliefs, but also to utilize Christians who have a high profile in the public square, for example professors of science who also believe in Jesus. This will allow us to speak in both spheres.

---

144. Dahle, "Apologetic Approach," 2.3.2, citing Guinness, "Mission in the Face of Modernity."

145. Dahle, "Apologetic Approach," 2.3.2, citing Newbigin, *Foolishness to the Greeks*, 10–18.

## Theological Background

Overall, it seems obvious that media and marketing theory (even the name is a giveaway of how close this is to the agora) should be used. Paul's example shows evangelists should know their audiences.

The next chapter will examine current audience research about our target demographic.

# 3

# Literature Review

This chapter considers recent attempts to measure and analyze religion and/or spirituality in Sydney.[1] From a dizzying array of alternatives, I will use as a working definition of spirituality the one used in interviews by Engebretson:

> Spirituality is: (a) *experience* of the sacred other which is accompanied by feelings of wonder, joy, love, trust and hope...(b) *connectedness* with and *responsibility* for the self, other people and the non-human world...(c) the *illumination* of lived experience with meaning and value...(d) the need for naming and *expression* in either traditional or non-traditional ways.[2]

---

1. Religion and spirituality are related concepts but not the same thing. Kathleen Engebretson differentiates religiosity (affiliation and public religious practice) from spirituality (more broad "appreciation of the sacred dimension in life" with implications for how one chooses to live). Engebretson, "Young People, Culture, and Spirituality."

2. Engebretson, "God's Got Your Back," 330.

*Literature Review*

## Seeing the City of Sydney

The Australian Survey of Social Attitudes, 2009, showed that 48% of Australians believe in God, but half of those are have doubts on the issue. In 1969, 87% believed in God.[3]

| Belief in God | % of Australian adults |
|---|---|
| I know God really exists and have no doubts about it | 25 |
| While I have doubts, I feel I do believe in God | 17 |
| I find myself believing in God, some of the time, but not others | 6 |
| I don't believe in a personal God, but I do believe in a spirit or life force | 20 |
| I don't know whether there is a God | 15 |
| I don't believe in God | 16 |

Source: Australian Survey of Social Attitudes (2009)[4]

Many commentators have noted that Australia is experiencing a decline in affiliation with mainstream Christian denominations, while also seeing some growth areas such as Hillsong, and also in the religions fed by immigration and in New Age religions.[5] The 2006 Census data reveals that traditional religion is in decline.

3. Hughes, *Shaping Australia's Spirituality*.
4. Hughes, *Australia's Religious Communities*.
5. Compare Possamai, *In Search of New Age Spiritualities*; Connell, "Hillsong."

## Asking Big Questions

Even though absolute numbers increased by over 100,000 in the period from 1996 to 2006, affiliation with Christian religions is falling as a proportion of the total population (from 71% in 1996 to 64% in 2006). Membership of Eastern religions such as Buddhism and Hinduism has increased dramatically in that period (from a low base and no doubt reflecting patterns of migration). And the proportion of the population with no religion rose in both absolute numbers (by 780,000) and as a proportion of the whole (from 17% in 1996 to 19% in 2010).[6] (It is recognized that some who list themselves as having no religion may describe themselves as spiritual. Yet many people say they have no idea what to think about God or religion or whether there is anything beyond: this group was 27% according to the Security and Wellbeing Survey,[7] compared with 14% who said there was nothing beyond and 16% who said there may be.) An analysis by Australian National University PhD candidate John Malcolm Armstrong suggests that while those Christians with low levels of attendance remained relatively constant from 1966 to 1996, the proportion of people with high levels of attendance declined, with more people attending services once a month rather than once a week.[8] This pattern continued into the twenty-first century according to data from the National Church Life Survey,[9] producing declines in attendance in most Christian churches.[10]

These results are challenging, even daunting, for a person of faith. Bouma reads them optimistically, arguing that Australians are not given to extroverted shows of religious sentiment, but do religion at "low temperature" or as a "shy hope in the heart," commenting that "not all things that evoke awe and wonder are

---

6. See also Salt, "Catholics vs. Nonbelievers," 29.
7. Kaldor et al., *Spirit Matters*, 49.
8. Armstrong, "Religious Attendance."
9. See National Church Life Survey, http://www.ncls.org.au.
10. See also Kaldor, *Build My Church*. It is recognized that church attendance is only one way of estimating spirituality, as it can be related to other variables, such as personality. See Kaldor et al., "Personality and Community Involvement," 101–5.

## Literature Review

loud and noisy, brassy and for sale."[11] Tacey also argues for an "upwelling of spiritual feeling in young people"[12] and looks for it in fresh forms relevant to Gen Y, despite their declining interest in traditional religions. Frame[13] reads the statistics as reflecting the reality that the indifferent and the downright hostile—whether called atheists, agnostics, rationalists or other names—have been ever with us.[14]

Sydney itself is very cosmopolitan, as Athens was in Paul's day. It is a leading arrival point for immigrants, and 52% of its population was born overseas or has a parent who was.[15] In a recent study of the geography of religious belief in Sydney, Stevenson and her colleagues[16] questioned the thesis of unidirectional secularization,[17] describing rather a process of secularization and desecularization happening at the same time and producing not the secular city of Harvey Cox[18] but a "post-secular city."[19] In summary, they found that

> largely because of its patterns of non-Christian immigration, the city is more religious (desecularised) than the rest of the country, even though Christianity has decreased and the "No Religion" category has grown since the Second World War.[20]

---

11. Bouma, *Australian Soul*, 2.

12. Tacey, *Spirituality Revolution*, 2; Tacey, *Re-enchantment*; Tacey, "What Spirituality Means." See also Collins, "Australians Quietly Spiritual."

13. Frame, *Losing My Religion*.

14. Hogan, "Australian Secularists," was one early analyst to see secularists as a subculture.

15. See Burnley, *Impact of Immigration*; Burnley, "Sydney's Changing Peoples."

16. Stevenson et al., "Religious Belief."

17. For a brief history and rather defensive critique of the secularisation thesis, see Borer, "New Atheism."

18. Cox, *Secular City*.

19. Stevenson et al., "Religious Belief," 324.

20. Ibid., 346.

They noted a "diversity in forms of non-belief." The census figures on which the study was based allows two categories in this area. The "No Religion" category fairly clearly includes agnostics, atheists, humanists and rationalists—anyone who has "made a conscious declaration of non-faith,"[21] accounting for 18.5% of Australians. Yet the second category, "Religious Affiliation Not Stated," includes people who did not answer this part of the census form. One can speculate about why this is so:[22] they may be spiritual in some sense but too "shy" to write on an official document about matters of faith, or they may simply be disinterested. Before the 2011 census, a rationalist group campaigned in the media for people to write "No Religion" if they currently had an affiliation that was merely traditional rather than active or heartfelt.[23] This was apparently led by a desire to lessen the faith statistics upon which politicians rely, as part of a campaign to militate against the religious right in politics,[24] and to separate church from state. However this group is explained, it accounts for 11% of Australians.

Stevenson and her colleagues analyzed census data according to four heuristic categories: Christian, Non-Christian, No Religion, and Religious Affiliation Not Stated. A summary of their analysis of every local government area (LGA) in Sydney shows that the Christian proportion declined in every LGA, and the non-Christian grew in all except one (namely, Leichhardt, the LGA that includes Balmain, the target audience for *Big Questions*, on which more later). The remaining categories were complex but broadly on the increase: of Sydney's forty-three LGAs, only eleven had a smaller proportion of No Religion and six had a smaller proportion of Religious Affiliation Not Stated. So secularization is strong in many parts of Sydney, often above the national average.[25]

21. Ibid., 332.

22. Engebretson confronts a similar question with teens, "God's Got Your Back," 335–37.

23. See censusnoreligion.org and census-campaign.org.au, and also census-campaign.org.uk.

24. Further, see Lohrey, "Voting for Jesus." Maddox, *God under Howard*.

25. Stevenson et al., "Religious Belief," 334.

*Literature Review*

Looking slightly more closely, the Christian proportion shows relatively high levels of decline in "the middle of the metropolitan area," running at 12% in the central Western LGAs which have received the most immigration since the 1980s: Parramatta, Holroyd, Auburn, Strathfield, and Burwood. The lowest declines in the Christian proportion are in peri-metropolitan LGAs like Hawkesbury, Ku-ring-gai, Camden, and Sutherland. The last two areas are "overwhelmingly Christian" (79% in Camden, 76% in Sutherland), well above the averages nationally and Sydney-wide (63%), and have been globally notorious as the site of a campaign to refuse an Islamic school near Camden, and of the 2005 Cronulla riots.[26] Some have referred to a "Bible belt" in Northwest Sydney, centered on Hillsong LGAs like Baulkham Hills (3% Pentecostals) and Blacktown (2% Pentecostals, compared to a Sydney-wide figure of 1%), but Stevenson and colleagues argue that this is a "dramatic exaggeration,"[27] as figures in these peri-metropolitan LGAs and others like them (Campbelltown, Hornsby, Penrith, Blue Mountains, Hawkesbury) show merely a somewhat slowed decline in Christianity, and secularism at a slower pace. In all Sydney LGAs except six the proportion not answering the question (Religious Affiliation Not Stated) grew between the 1996 and 2006 censuses, and Stevenson and her colleagues interpret this as "faith shyness"; the countertrending six LGAs these include Baulkham Hills, as well as peri-metropolitans like Hornsby, Ku-ring-gai, and Blue Mountains, and they see these as the least faith-shy areas of Sydney, attributing Pentecostalism and the Uniting Church.[28] Leichhardt, by contrast, is among the most faith-shy.

The non-religious segment has increased in three quarters of Sydney's LGAs between the 1996 and 2006 censuses, and this is strongest in the Inner West: Leichhardt, Marrickville, and Hurstville, according to Stevenson and her colleagues. These were high immigration reception sites since WWII, and have gentrified since

---

26. Ibid., 340. On the issue of inter-group relations, see Bouma, "Emergence of Religious Plurality."

27. Stevenson et al., "Religious Belief," 344.

28. Ibid.

the 1980s. Leichhardt recorded the highest proportion of those identifying as nonbelievers (26.7%) and the steepest rate of growth in this sector (8.7%). Closely following these Inner West areas were the affluent northern and inner suburbs, where around 20% of people were atheists or of no religion: Manly, Mosman, North Sydney, City of Sydney, Lane Cove, and Willoughby.

> Belief in these areas comes closest to the expected secularism of modernist society and of cosmopolitan world cities. These are areas of gentrification cosmopolitanism, higher levels of university education, and the affluent middle-class "globals."[29]

Stevenson and her colleagues divided Sydney into "five broad geographies":

1. Areas influenced by non-Christian migration, in which the decline in Christianity is countered by an increase in non-Christian religions, particularly Islam and to a lesser extent Buddhism. This is the most numerous group, and is most noticeable in Auburn, Fairfield, Parramatta, Blacktown and Liverpool. Yet these areas also saw a modest rise in the non-religious proportion.

2. The so-called Bible belt, where "the decline of Christianity has been stalled by the growth in new Christian faiths (Pentecostals), by the robustness of smaller denominations (Uniting Church), and incipient growth in the non-Christian presence."[30] The researchers note that this is not linked simply to immigration, but probably with "value shifts" or a decline in trust and satisfaction with established Christian groups.[31]

3. Low change areas. These affluent areas of Sydney's Northern Beaches and North Shore have been little affected by recent immigration. Here, a small decline in the Christian proportion is explained by a rise in the non-Christian and non-religious proportions, about half each.

29. Ibid., 343–44.
30. Ibid., 345.
31. Ibid., 346.

*Literature Review*

4. The Eastern Suburbs has large cultural overlap with the last group mentioned, being affluent and less affected by recent immigration, with the addition that Randwick and Waverly LGAs have a longstanding Jewish presence. (One notes that one North Shore area surrounding St. Ives would fit best into this category, however these authors note exceptions and micro-geographies underlying the broad trends they describe). Another key difference is that these areas have seen a steep decline in the proportion of Christians, matched by increases not in the non-Christians but in the non-religious.

5. Cosmopolitan Sydney. This includes Leichhardt, Marrickville, City of Sydney and Hurstville.

> Proportions of Christians in these areas are declining, and there is only minimal growth of the presence of non-Christians. In these areas atheism is very robust, and the expansion of the decidedly non-religious outstrips even the presence and growth of the faith shy. This geographical section of inner and inner-western Sydney provides the clearest example of secularisation, and of the retreat of faith in modern Western cities.[32]

One could attempt to relate these geographies to Caldwell's Eight Tribes, but only in broad approximations. Stevenson's first geography might include Bankstown and Cabramatta. The second might include some from North Shore but even some around Baulkham Hills and Windsor whose values are similar to those of the Toowoomba tribe, and indeed it could be argued that Caldwell's model does not describe the Hills as well as it might. The third is fairly clearly the North Shore tribe, plus some people on the Northern beaches whose cultural values have some overlap with Byron Bay. The fourth could coincide with Vaucluse. The fifth is the Balmain tribe.

32. Ibid.

The first two groups above are examples of de-secularization: "immigrant Sydney" and "Bible belt" Sydney.³³ Overall, Sydney could be characterized "either as a post-secular city of increasing non-Christian faith, or as a post-Christian city."³⁴ And our chosen demographic is in some ways the most resistant to the idea of God, and the most challenging. Marketing theory would suggest one should target "low-hanging fruit" first, namely those demographics which are most easily reachable and will bring profits that may fund efforts to other demographics. Yet the Christian is called to "go into all the world and preach the gospel" (Mark 16:15).

It seems fair to say that the forces of secularization are "dramatically uneven across Sydney,"³⁵ and it would be fascinating to theorize in more detail as to why. This research can provide a wide establishing shot of religion in Australia, but invites close-up consideration of details, and particularly of the reasoning and experience behind people's decisions for or against the existence and relevance of God. Stevenson and colleagues acknowledge that census data on affiliation and non-affiliation cannot measure the strength of religious convictions, and "the nature and spatial patterning of the performance of religion and its behaviours."³⁶ Why are individuals religious or non-religious? How closely does this correlate to being spiritual or non-spiritual? Are these people open to spirituality if it is presented in terms acceptable to them? Our research in chapter 4 below will begin exploring this gap.

## Toward In-Depth Research: A Pilot Study

While national quantitative data can provide aggregate information, there is a role for in-depth research, particularly interviews, to fill out key details and zoom in on individual reasoning processes.

33. Ibid., 345.
34. Ibid., 346.
35. Ibid.
36. Ibid., 347.

*Literature Review*

Previous to the research project at the center of this present Doctor of Ministry project, I co-commissioned a pilot study[37] by Windshift, highly regarded as a leading niche provider of social research and market research. In a study co-funded by a corporate player in the FMCG sector, Windshift conducted in-depth interviews to ask a group of Australians whether they believed in God and why. What was filling their spiritual void (if any)? What was sacred to them? What virtues do they value most? How do they talk about the meaning of life? What mysteries occur to them? What is their sense of connection with the universe, the earth, other people? What sense of purpose do they have? And what beliefs support them through crises and tragedies?

This research aimed to understand how members of different tribes perceive their spiritual needs, and find out what is filling the spiritual void for those with low or no attendance at church, with a view to targeting a documentary series. We interviewed eleven Sydney residents from a range of socio-economic backgrounds broadly corresponding to the tribes and representing four religious traditions: Christianity (7), Hinduism (2), Islam (1), Judaism (1), though only one attended public worship monthly or more and four attended for high or holy days, while six did not attend except for social obligations (other people's weddings and funerals). Here is a summary of sample characteristics:

---

37. Caldwell, "Australian Spirituality: A Pilot Report," unpublished report delivered to Cathy McDonald and Grenville Kent, May 2010, 7.

## Asking Big Questions

| Number of Interviews | 11 |
|---|---|

### Personal Values [more than 1 tribe per person]

| | |
|---|---|
| Byron Bay | 2 |
| Bankstown | 4 |
| Balmain | 4 |
| Toowoomba | 2 |
| Cabramatta | 3 |
| North Shore | 6 |

### Age

| | |
|---|---|
| 18 to 35 | 4 |
| 35 to 64 | 7 |
| Over 65 | 0 |

### Gender

| | |
|---|---|
| Male | 5 |
| Female | 6 |

### Religious Adherence

| | |
|---|---|
| Church most months | 1 |
| Church occasionally / at one time but not currently | 6 |
| No religious practice | 4 |

### Education

| | |
|---|---|
| Uni degree or higher | 6 |
| TAFE/Vocational | 3 |
| No tertiary | 2 |

*Literature Review*

Most respondents were in the unsure middle on the question of God:

## Belief in God

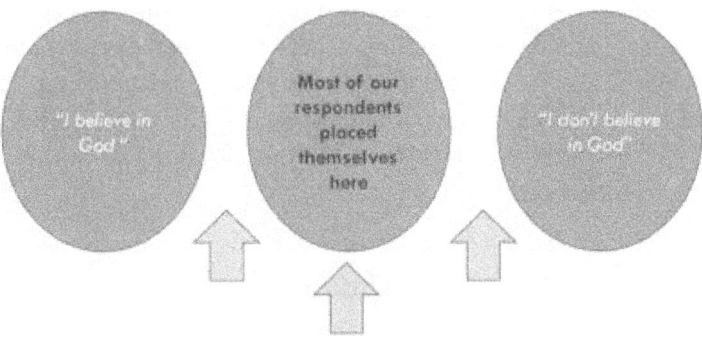

When respondents were asked their reasons for and against belief, they gave the following list:

Factors inclining toward belief:
- God has answered my prayers—it is a two way street
- When good things happen, I thank God
- Belief in a power that protects, supports, and guides you
- Holy day celebrations—Easter, Christmas reinforce belief
- Family belief
- My values (caring, supportive, appreciative, hard working)

Factors inclining toward disbelief:
- Religious extremity, rigidity & rules
- War
- Hard times test faith
- When bad things keep happening to me despite the fact that "I am a good person"

## Asking Big Questions

- Hypocrisy of religious people
- Doesn't fit with my life focus[38]

It should be acknowledged that my initial questions about reasoning processes tended (obviously, in retrospect) to privilege reason. Yet the answers revealed that there was more than "reasoning" going on. This became evident as the first interview progressed and, thanks to a responsive and perceptive interviewer, led to a new axis which was beyond my initial model. (This is what a pilot study is meant to do.) It yielded the following grid (with key representative quotes from participants):

## Relationship with God[39]

Our sample differed strongly in terms of the level of certainty they had in their spiritual beliefs and, markedly, in the extent to which their relationship with God was personal and emotional or philosophical and intellectual.

|  | Certainty |  |
|---|---|---|
| Personal | "God is in the back seat of my car" | "Everything happens for a reason – it is related to deeds or karma" |
|  | "If there is a God, I'm praying. If there isn't, I'm just talking to myself" | "I believe in some kind of higher power... You see evidence of it in the little mysteries" | Philosophical
|  | Uncertainty |  |

This finding provides a valuable corrective to "argumentative" apologetics. It suggests that deft apologetic approaches will consider people's personal experiences and intuitions and work

---

38. Caldwell, "Australian Spirituality," 19.
39. Ibid., 9.

# Literature Review

with those, which is much more wholistic than merely persuading the rational side of a person (important though that is).

## Pathways to Belief

These interviewees spoke of three primary pathways to belief in God.[40] The first involved religious schooling, which, though it may have left people with a jumbled understanding of religion, seemed often to have laid the groundwork for a belief in God which they retained. A religious family—especially if it was a migrant family—also seemed to leave an indelible impression, even if its adult children did not maintain its religious practice.[41] There was also one instance of a "born again" Christian who had experienced an epiphany at a low point in his life. This person had attended church as a child, but currently did not regularly attend.

| Religious schooling | Religious family | Religious epiphany |
| --- | --- | --- |
| Observance | Expectation | Conviction |
| Agnosticism | Community | |
| Incompleteness | Compartmentalisation | Born Again |
| Fuzziness | Hypocrisy | |

---

40. This question of coming to faith touches on theological debates on how much evidence is involved. Clark, "How Real People Believe," argues that, according to Reformed epistemology, belief in God does not require evidence—that is, a propositional argument or theistic proof—in order to be rational. This is a fascinating discussion, but it is outside the scope of this thesis.

41. Compare Warner and Williams, "Role of Families."

# Asking Big Questions

## Values, Concepts, and "Brands"

Respondents were given three word-sort exercises aimed at identifying the spiritual values and religious concepts they value, and their perceptions of religious "brands."

Their top 16 words from the 36 word list of spiritual values were:

### Spiritual Values

Hope, Joy, Love

Care, Compassion, Faith, Gratitude, Intelligence, Nature, Well-Being

Believe, Creativity, Goodness, Moral, Purpose, Wonder

From a list of forty-two words about religious practice, they rated these most highly:

### Religious Concepts

Charity

Karma

God, Heaven, Morality, Soul, Teachings, Virtues

Ceremony prayer

Of 32 words denoting religious "brands," the most commonly selected was "God." Note that though there were no practising Buddhists in the sample, Buddha and Buddhism rated relatively highly.

| Religion Brands |
| --- |
| God |
| Christian, Jesus |
| Buddhism |
| Bible |
| Buddha, Catholic, Dalai Lama |

Jehovah's Witnesses had the least favorable response. No one selected Seventh-day Adventists or Presbyterians.

## Perceptions of Believers, Nonbelievers, and Religion

When asked to describe believers, most people provided a mix of positives and negatives—principled and caring on the one hand; earnest, judgemental and less independent on the other.

# Asking Big Questions

## Believers

### Positive/Neutral

- Family people, hard working, honest, caring, look out for others
- Value institution of marriage
- Value fairness, not doing harm, the "good"
- Have a foundation—principles to live by

### Negative

- "Goody-goodies"
- Earnest, boring
- Judgmental
- May think there is only one way to live
- Don't think for themselves—followers

Surprisingly to me, nonbelievers were seen more negatively by this largely uncommitted sample group, who perceived more cynicism and less caring and connection.

## Nonbelievers

### Positive/Neutral

- More free—not restricted by rules, "shoulds"
- Academic / scientific
- Logical

### Negative

- Unrooted, chameleons
- Cynical, hard, angry
- Not from a good family
- Run with a bad crowd
- Less meaning or purpose—sense of missing out

Note, however, that nonbelievers owned the territory of logic, academia, and science. Faith and science were seen to be in conflict, rather than different ways of seeing the world.[42]

## Perceptions of Religion

### Positive/Neutral

- Ceremonies, architecture
- Hymns
- Family, community
- Guiding principles

---

42. In this connection, see Plantinga, "Religion and Science," *Stanford Encyclopedia of Philosophy*, http://plato.stanford.edu/entries/religion-science.

### Negative

- Leads to conflict & division
- "The religious part of religion is a no-no to me—too many hypocrisies"
- Wanting to convert me
- People judging me
- Flawed people being "holier than thou"
- Out of touch with modern life

Religion itself also had a fairly negative perception—its principles and ceremonies were appreciated (and one respondent said a nice Gothic church added to property values in the area!), but its combination of judgement and hypocrisy was too much for most, and it was seen as mired in the past.

## What Spiritual Void?

Our respondents clearly have spiritual ideals. Yet they see believers and religions generally as judgmental, a little out of step with contemporary life and hypocritical. So where do they meet their spiritual needs? Where do they celebrates hope, love and joy, when these personal spiritual beliefs seem to have separated themselves from religious practice? We considered what specifically religions have traditionally provided—purpose in life, help in crisis, and universal truth—and then asked our semi-believing respondents where they found these.

## Personal Purpose in Life

This proved to be a good question in terms of establishing people's values and priorities. Typically those with young families were focused on their children. Others were still searching or saw their purpose being fulfilled by their work. Goodness and charity was also considered to be elements of purpose. Broadly, the categories of response were:

- More of what I'm doing now.
- First make money, so I can then honor my family.
- Role/identity focus
    - be a good person
    - provide for my family
- Instrumental focus
    - make good use of what I've been given—my life, talents, gifts
    - give to and learn from others
- I'm still searching
    - but my life currently does feel meaningful
- Purpose has to arrive, and can't be constructed

## Help in Crisis

In stress and crisis, our respondents saw pros and cons to involving God. It would be nice to believe God was caring for us, but then in fairness we would also have to blame God for specific bad things that happened, and that seemed to negate the effect, so some chose to do neither. (In my words, the problem of evil is impacting on their doctrine of providence.) Others were more likely to establish cause and effect for both the good and bad things and to make their "belief" contingent on outcomes.

## Asking Big Questions

Broadly, the categories of response were:
- Personal Focus
    - I am a good person
    - I am grateful for all I have been given
- Broad Principles
    - What goes around, comes around. Popularized Karma.
    - Negative experiences are a test of character
- Spiritual Focus
    - I am being watched over—by loved ones, by God?

### What Fills the Spiritual Void?

Summarizing the responses produces a list of different ways people seem to fill their own spiritual void—though they would not speak of it in these terms because they do not think about spirituality much at all, but rather subsume it into different aspects of life and do not worry about it. These other areas are:
- Focus on family
- Focus on achievement
- Personal creativity
- Busyness
- Shopping
- Being a good person / doing good
- Having fun
- A sense of self-assurance & self-awareness
- Other beliefs, e.g., karma

## Universal Truth

What of curiosity about life's big questions? Wonder is an important spiritual value for these research participants, and yet this is not really wonder about the infinite universe. They simply accept that they don't know—or can't know. When we ask them, "Is there a mind/spirit behind the universe?," they show more mild curiosity or indifference than genuine wonder. Some verbalized the question of whether the cause was a big bang or God—or some synthesis. They were left with more questions than answers as to "what is outside the outside." One respondent said, "I don't go there. I don't think as broadly as the universe." However nature, rather than the universe, seems to be their larger whole. They appreciate the natural world and sometimes feel awe at being part of such a great whole, feeling that they should not take it for granted, and that changes in nature act as warning signals.

In connection with notions of truth, Hughes has argued that students' approach to religious knowledge contrasts with their approach to other kinds of knowledge.[43] He found students hold a diverse range of opinions, often with a lack of clarity and many "maybes," and assume that each person can shop for individual beliefs from various sources, and can legitimately form their own beliefs. He argues that postmodern relativism is applied more to religion than to other subjects, and produces "Whateverism."[44] The comments of our respondents seemed to reflect similar attitudes. Hughes' comment is:

> Religion remains in the grey edge of the world of knowledge. Any attempt to teach it as if it were similar to science, history, or other forms of knowledge only encounters resistance.[45]

In summary, our respondents indicated a crisis in the social aspects of religion, suspicion of any hint of selling or pushing

---

43. Hughes, "Characteristics of Religious Knowledge," 137–47.
44. Hughes, "Characteristics of Religious Knowledge," 145.
45. Ibid., 147.

views, and a diminished need or respect for religious institutions and leaders. They felt little sense of spiritual void, though were attracted to some concepts and words with a traditional religious connections. They showed little interest in the universe or truth, but were comfortable with mystery.

Is this the great age of spirituality, a ripe field for Christian sowing? Some have seen tremendous possibilities[46] yet other researchers are less sanguine.[47] Rather than a generation of motivated spiritual seekers, Generation Y could be best characterized as agnostic.[48] So Christians should not imagine noble urbanites doing by nature the things contained in the law, or benighted souls looking heavenward for some ray of light or awaiting the missionary with the water of life. They are getting on with life in one of the world's premier cities, making up pragmatic, pleasure-maximizing rules and occasional patches of worldview as they go, perhaps not even noticing that they are thirsty. A Christian would assume that they have massive spiritual needs, but they may not even feel them. This has tremendous parallels with Athens. Nobody came to Paul begging to be taught Christianity—he had to venture into the marketplace and attract attention as best he could. Capturing the interest of secular people today with a Christian message is still extremely difficult, and will require (under God) careful consideration and research, which will be attempted in the following chapter.

---

46. One thinks of Drane, *What Is the New Age*; Croft et al., *Evangelism in a Spiritual*.

47. Riddell, *Threshold of the Future*; Savage et al., *Making Sense of Generation Y*.

48. Mason et al., *Spirit of Generation Y*, 11.

# 4

## Qualitative Research and Interpretation

### Research Method

IN-DEPTH INTERVIEWS WERE SELECTED because they are arguably the best qualitative method for uncovering "underlying motivations, beliefs, attitudes and feelings on a topic."[1] They leave the interviewer free to probe carefully into issues, particularly layered, emotive, or sensitive issues which may involve social pressure and where respondents may feel pressure to conform if they were in a group situation such as a focus group,[2] particularly on issues to do with the private life.[3] These heavily depend on the skill and lack of bias of the interviewer,[4] and can be the most expensive way to conduct interviews,[5] but they allow depth and freedom in answers. These interviews were structured by a moderator's guide, and parts of this comprised a "structured, undis-

1. Malhotra, *Marketing Research*, 146.
2. Churchill, *Marketing Research*, 287. Malhotra, *Marketing Research*, 148.
3. Burns and Bush, *Marketing Research*, 251.
4. Cf. the interviewer-interviewee interaction model, which considers this. Churchill, *Marketing Research*, 594–95.
5. Ibid., 310.

guised questionnaire," where certain questions were presented in exactly the same words. This standardization makes the study repeatable, because another interviewer asking the same questions should produce similar answers from the respondents (assuming they had not changed their attitudes).[6] Personal interviews can provide quality control difficulties for the manager,[7] but in this case the interviews were audio recorded for checking.

Thirteen interviews of approximately one hour in duration were conducted for this research project. Nine of these were conducted face-to-face in a cafe location in the Sydney CBD, and four by telephone. Participants were paid standard industry rates. The purpose was to gain qualitative insights into the attitudes and perceptions of the Balmain Tribe toward the notions of God and Christianity.

Below is a copy of the moderator's guide to conducting the in-depth interviews:

## In-Depth Interviews—Moderators Guide

*First, thanks so much for meeting up with me today. We'll just be chatting today for about an hour about your thoughts toward belief systems, and in particular, God and Christianity. Please be assured that I am from an independent research company, and while I understand a few things we're discussing today can be seen as quite personal, everything you talk about today will be strictly confidential and for research purposes only.*

### Initial (20 minutes)

- Where do you feel spirituality is at in Australia today? (What about compared to 5 years ago? Stronger or weaker) What role does it play in our society vs. individual life? (None to a lot)

6. Ibid., 285.
7. Ibid., 310.

## Qualitative Research and Interpretation

- Would you classify yourself as a spiritual person? (Yes, definitely. Yes, somewhat. No.)
- Elements which incline you 1. toward / 2. away from a belief in a personal God:
    - Intuitions / feelings / a sense
    - Experiences
    - Perceptions / observations
    - Lines of argument / logic / philosophy and knowledge
- Going through each of the above, how strong do you think these are (out of 10)?
- So it sounds like there are some personal thoughts in there, as well as some philosophical and scientific—how do you balance all these aspects or fit them together? Do some aspects hold more weight than others?
- How important do you find the question of God's existence? Has this changed at various times in your life? Why?
    - Foundational
    - Substantial Significant (it matters, just like other significant things)
    - Peripheral
    - Not at all
- What do you see as your purpose in life? Is there a overall purpose in life? Is there a universal purpose? How did you arrive at this?
- What do you think of the person of Jesus? (He didn't exist, Real person but not divine, Real person and divine, Real person, divine and son of God)
- What do you think about his:

## Asking Big Questions

- Frequently spending time with the outcasts of society (the lame, the poor, women)
- Claims to be the Son of God
- Miracles
- Death on the cross
- Resurrection

• What helps you through crisis and uncertainty? What place does religion play? (What fills the traditional place of religion in your life?)

• What words or phrases come to mind when you think about people who practice a religion? Who are Christians who regularly attend church? Follower of Jesus, Born again Christians, evangelical?

- How do you think other Australians like yourself view Christians?

• What characteristics do you associate with people who don't believe in God?

• Do you think that non-belief or belief makes a difference to how a person lives? How?

## Watch video (2 mins)

• Assess Thoughts on "Big Questions" (10 mins)

- Ask before and after how interested they are/would be in this DVD.
- Initial thoughts, interest in watching this

## 1. Read Arguments for/against Existence of God (25 mins)

1. To what extent do you agree/disagree (strongly, somewhat, somewhat, strongly)

## Qualitative Research and Interpretation

2. *Does this argument incline you toward, or away from the belief in a personal God? How much of an issue is it in terms of blocking your belief in the existence of God?*
3. *Have you heard any plausible or coherent responses to this issue? Have you heard any rebuttals?*

a. The fact that people suffer suggests there cannot be a God who is wise, kind and strong enough to stop it. (The Problem of Pain.)
b. The existence of superb engineering in nature (e.g., a bird's flying technologies) suggests an Engineer. (The Design Argument). The incredible language-like complexity and "spelling" of DNA (3.5 billion chemical letters, compared to 130,000 for Hamlet) suggests an Author. (The Design Argument). The fact that so many factors went right for planet Earth to support human life, plus that so many Physics variables are at just the right settings for the universe to exist, suggests a God. (The Fine Tuning Argument) Show clip from BQs (e.g. Bird's wings)
c. (The Problem of Hell) How could a loving God allow people to go to hell?
d. The universe could not have kick-started itself, so there must be something outside it. (The Cosmological Argument)
e. (The Problem of the Supernatural) I can't believe in a God who deals in angels, resurrections, walking on water, miracles and demons.
f. The human mind is more than the physical brain, and cannot be explained as a product of a universe that has only matter and no mind elsewhere in it or behind it. A better explanation would be a larger Mind, i.e. God, giving us consciousness. (The Argument from Consciousness.) Yearning for spiritual answers.
g. There are moral absolutes. (e.g., It is never morally right to rape. It is never right to senselessly torture a child or an animal.) We cannot get moral absolutes from nature (because the

jungle is about survival of the fittest and my "selfish genes," not altruism or loving my neighbour). Historically, the only place humans have found moral absolutes is in the idea of a God who holds me accountable for how I treat my neighbour and cares about everyone. (The Moral Argument)

---

At first, interviewees were asked to answer open questions, and the interviewer briefed to avoid "leading the witness." After that, they were asked to read brief statements of some of the classic arguments for and against God's existence, and to express their response. Recognizing that a few lines of text may not do justice to a subtle argument, the interviewer checked whether they had understood it and, if needed, explained it more (without obvious advocacy). Then their responses were sought. Key comments were noted on a soft copy of the above form, and the audio of each entire interview was digitally recorded, and later transcribed for analysis.

After the initial in-depth interviews, participants were given a copy of the *Big Questions* DVD (duration 28 mins) and instructed verbally to watch it in their own time and complete an online survey which took approximately 4 minutes to complete, for which they would be mailed a gift voucher as a further incentive. A copy of the survey is bellow:

## Survey: *Big Questions* DVD

1. Did you watch the DVD through in one sitting? (Yes/No. Space for comment.)
2. How interesting was it? (Extremely, very, somewhat, slightly, not at all. Space for comment.)
3. How entertaining was it? (Extremely, very, somewhat, slightly, not at all. Space for comment.)
4. How believable and compelling was its content and message? (Extremely, very, somewhat, slightly, not at all. Space for comment.)
5. Overall, how enjoyable was *Big Questions*? (Extremely, very, somewhat, slightly, not at all. Space for comment.)
6. Before watching this film, how likely would you have been to watch another documentary like *Big Questions*? (Not at all, slightly, somewhat, very. Space for comment.)
7. After watching this film, how likely would you be to watch another documentary like *Big Questions*? (Not at all, slightly, somewhat, very. Space for comment.)
8. Would you recommend this film to friends? (Definitely, probably, no. Space for comment.)
9. What aspects or parts of the documentary did you like and think worked well? (Space for comment.)
10. What aspects of parts of the documentary did you think should be improved? (Space for comment.)
11. What other topics should be treated in the rest of this series? (Space for comment.)

A link to this survey was emailed to the participants in the following days as a reminder. Participants were given ten days to complete the online survey, and twelve of the thirteen respondents did so.

## Asking Big Questions

Having trained and worked as a market researcher and taught marketing research, I would have liked to conduct the interviews myself. However, the research centered on the pilot episode of a film series in which I am the presenter, and at one point in the interview a brief excerpt of the film was played to illustrate the argument from design. For this reason, doing my own interviewing would have been inadvisable because it may well have created demand artefacts in the results. For example, it would have been harder for interviewees to criticize aspects of my film to my face. It could also have created perceived biases, where interviewees and readers of the research could question my objectivity and professional distance in hearing and analyzing the results. So I contracted McCrindle Research, who sent researcher Hester Kahei to conduct the interviews and summarize the data in conjunction with research directors Claire Madden and Mark McCrindle. This project benefited from input and analysis from experienced market and social researchers, who suggested questions I would not have asked and saw things in the data that I would have missed, and expressed it in apt phrases which I have often borrowed here. However, I also did my own careful analysis. I was able to access audio recordings and their transcriptions, and to read the interviewer's notes.

## Sample Selection

Participants were selected based on their similarity to descriptors of the Balmain Tribe (see the Project Description: Target Audience section in chap. 1). Interview participants generally satisfied this criterion. Most lived in a location close to Sydney CBD, and those who lived further away were selected due to their frequency of visit to Balmain, Newtown, Surry Hills, and Paddington. Interviewees were intellectual in orientation, most holding a minimum of a bachelor's degree. They were characterized by their interest in frequenting inner-city cafes, vegan/vegetarian eateries, independent cinemas, non-mainstream bookshops, growers' markets, and urban markets while also shopping at gourmet delis and upmarket

## Qualitative Research and Interpretation

grocery stories, and attending cultural events like film festivals and public lectures. Ten of the thirteen interviewees were from Generation Y (aged 18–31).

*Identifiers were as follows:*

| Gender | |
|---|---|
| Male | 7 |
| Female | 6 |

| Age | |
|---|---|
| 18–31 | 10 |
| 32–46 | 1 |
| 47–65 | 2 |

Though this is not quantitative research, participants were selected to be broadly representative of the Balmain tribe in religion: that is, a majority of people of no religion, including people with background affiliation in mainstream religions but no or low current attendance. Their religious views were as follows:

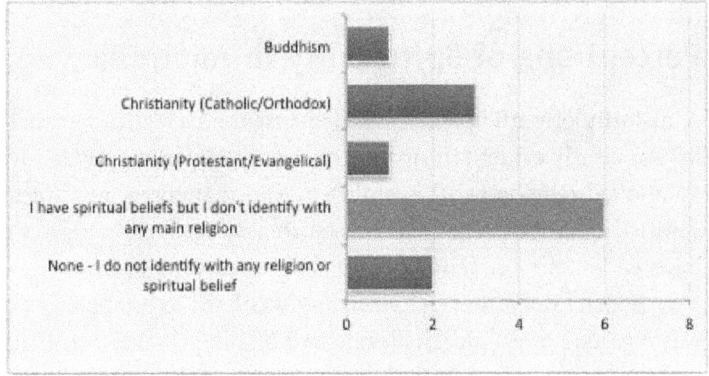

Most participants did not identify with the Christian faith, and none of the four who described themselves as Christian was attending worship services regularly (i.e. monthly or more). A significant number of participants thought Christians should be afforded religious freedom, but did not wish to be involved in Christianity themselves. Their attitudes to Christianity were as follows:

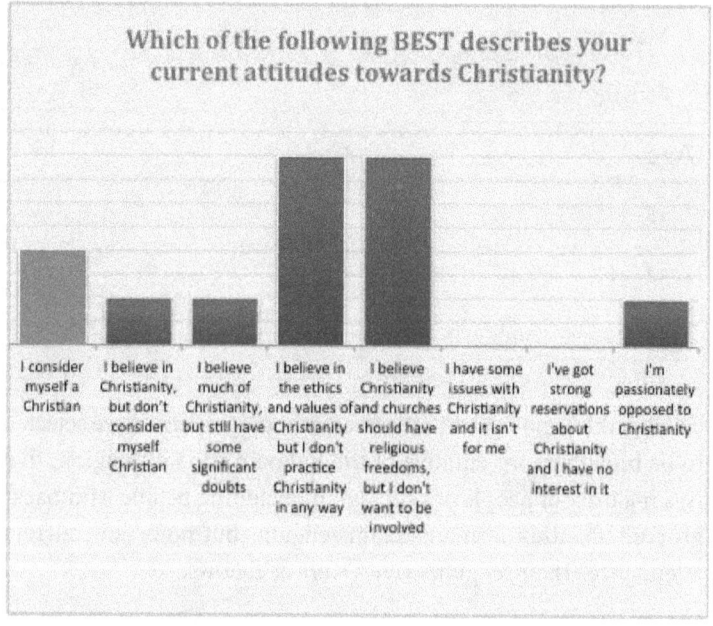

## Perceptions of Spirituality in Australia

A majority of participants indicated that they felt that spirituality was clearly evident in Australian society. However they hardly mentioned religion at all, seeming to find it almost irrelevant to spiritual questions. They viewed spirituality and religion as two independent notions, and thought about them differently.

A strict definition of spirituality was hard to establish, as it was regarded as a fluid, malleable and highly personal construct with a strong sense of their ability to "pick and choose" what they

## Qualitative Research and Interpretation

believed. Only a minority of participants felt they currently had solid, logical evidence underlying their beliefs.

As a general trend, those who expressed that they themselves were not religious or spiritual often tended to indicate that they felt that society was more spiritual than they were, while those who claimed to be religious or spiritual tended to indicate that society as a whole was less spiritual than they were. This is expressed graphically below:

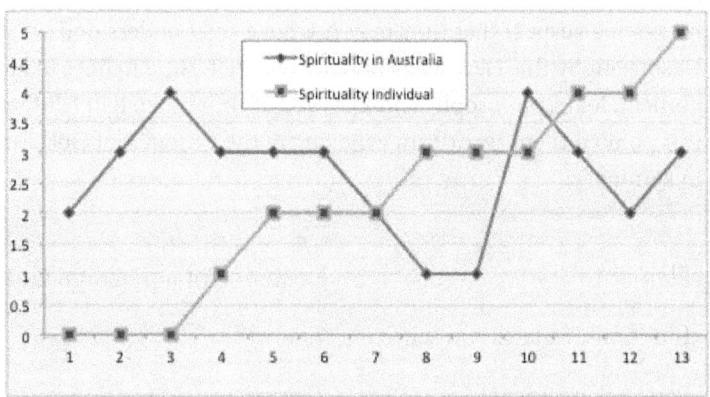

Overall, they also perceived themselves as less spiritual than average. On aggregate figures, spirituality was rated at 2.6 (out of a maximum of 5), whereas respondents' own individual spirituality was at 2.2.

## Factors Driving Belief and Unbelief: Rationality Trumps

When asked about their beliefs regarding the existence of a personal God, participants' viewpoints were varied. In an effort to uncover the individual factors driving belief and unbelief, they were asked to indicate whether a list of elements inclined them toward or away from believing in a personal God. The list was:

85

## Asking Big Questions

1. Intuitions, feelings and inner sense
2. Personal experiences
3. Perceptions and observations
4. Lines of argument, logic, philosophy and knowledge

Generally, they felt the first two elements—their intuitions, feelings, and inner sense, and also their personal experiences—inclined them toward believing in a personal God. The third element, comprising observations and perceptions, included just over half of our respondents toward belief. (The split answer here makes me suspect that they may not have fully understood what was meant by this element.) However, when it came to lines of argument, logic, philosophy and knowledge, more than half felt that this pointed them away from believing in the existence of God. So, in summary:

| Element | Existence of a personal God |
| --- | --- |
| Intuitions, feelings and sense | *Toward* |
| Personal experiences | *Toward* |
| Perceptions and observations | *Either way* |
| Lines of argument, logic, philosophy and knowledge | *Away* |

So if they feel that various lines of evidence point in both directions, how do they weigh the various elements and decide whether to believe in a personal God? They were asked how they weight feelings and reason, and responses were as follows:

## Qualitative Research and Interpretation

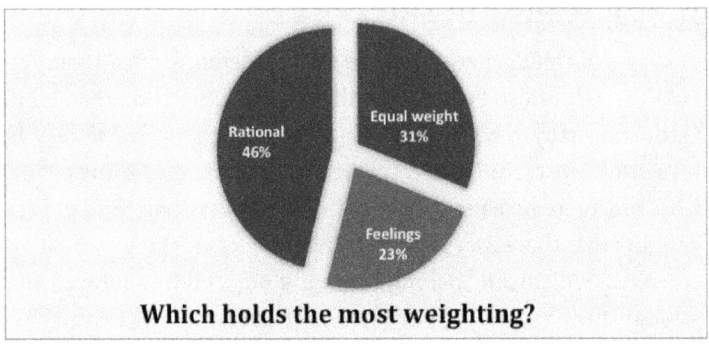

**Which holds the most weighting?**

In three out of four elements, people felt some inclination toward belief in God, but allowed a rational objection to override this. Reason is the top or equal top factor driving just over three-quarters of their spiritual views (remembering that this is qualitative research rather than quantitative). One could also say that emotion is top or equal factor in just over half. (Of course, psychologists and philosophers could debate whether people really know their own motivation or pride ourselves on being more rational or emotionally intelligent than we really are, but in this study we can only deal with their self-perceptions.)

Our respondents seem to have gained the impression that most intellectuals—scientists in particular—do not have space for God in their worldviews, and that atheists own the perception of rationality (see the Perceptions of Believers, Nonbelievers, and Religion section in chap. 3).

## Implications

These findings are crucial to the central aim of *Big Questions*. Simply put, we aim to give intellectual permission to rational people who would like to believe. This aim is partly based on pastoral observation that many young people raised in the church seem to lose their faith at university, and also that educated people can often take longer to come to faith and need a lot of things explained reasonably before they will then begin to exercise faith as a quasi-evidence of things that cannot be seen or demonstrated (compare Heb 11:1). It is also built on the theological conviction that, while God is in many ways ineffable and much of the universe may be mysterious to mere human intellects, there are also things about God which are revealed and may be known rationally and experientially: that there are "hidden things" but also "things which are revealed," which can "belong to us and our children forever, that we may do all the ideas of this *torah*." (Deut 29:29). There are ways in which humans cannot search out God (Job 11:7), but ways in which we can search and find if we search with our whole selves (Jer 29:13–14). While natural theologies are ever vulnerable to the flaws in human reason—hubris, passion, self-bias—human reason can be used to consider evidence in the natural world which, rightly interpreted, points to God. And so I wish to respond to the New Atheist claim to be "Brights" (see the Some New Thing from "the Sparrow" section in chap. 2), and demonstrate that Christianity has deep logic and that many Christians are highly intelligent and educated and curious. At a practical level, this means using interviews with top professors who are also people of faith, and not merely personal faith hidden in the private domain acceptable to modernism, but finding hints and pointers to God in the center of their academic disciplines in the public domain. They need to give the best rational arguments for theism, and at the same time embody the truth that one can believe in God and be a "Bright." Oxford Professor John Lennox briefly considers the question of how many theists and atheists are and have been at the top levels of science.[8]

In short, this is rational persuasion, demonstrating that there are logical reasons to believe in God with the mind. This is Paul's major approach in Athens, and it is still relevant. So much of what is called evangelism seems to me to be targeting the "Bible Belt," trying to rekindle the faith of lapsed Christians, rather than going to the agora and the Areopagus and giving reasons to believe. Yet Paul is not the only prophet to tell us to give an *apologia* (case,

8. Lennox, *God's Undertaker*, 17–30.

## Qualitative Research and Interpretation

verbal defense) for the hope that we have (1 Pet 3:15), and to do so with gentleness and respect rather than the arrogance sometimes associated with modernism.

Yet a second important strategy is to give these reasons in a way that awakens wonder and curiosity, and provokes further questioning. For example, our research suggests that people adore nature and particularly animals, and find it evocative of childlike awe. Yet I have the sense that this must be done in a restrained way. Too much "emotionalism" would instantly arouse the intellectual security guards of suspicion and rationalism as a defense. The Balmain Tribe is marked by its intellectualism, and I do not believe that we can find a way into their hearts if we do not have permission from their heads. Stated more positively, they can become quite emotional but only if they are convinced and their reason respected.

This is part of the reason I have chosen to involve a child as my co-presenter. This was not just an excuse to do some great travel with my son Marcus; it was a deliberate strategy to allow certain questions to be asked from a childlike angle. For example, in episode 1, Marcus makes the observation, "An Airbus comes from these huge factories. An albatross comes from one egg." I find this a telling comparison, and many audience members laugh during screenings and see the comparison which actually shows the incredible superiority of natural technology. Yet I also have a sense that the line would not work coming from me, and that I needed to stay in the logical adult world and let Marcus embody curiosity and wide-eyed openness to the numinous in the film. I also had the sense that having a child in the film would remove acrimony from the debate. Then again, after Richard Dawkins's much-publicized comments about religion brainwashing children,[9] I needed to be careful to keep Marcus curious about nature rather than

---

9. Cf. Dawkins, *God Delusion*, chap. 9, "Childhood, Abuse and the Escape from Religion." Professor Dawkins has personally contributed to a summer camp for atheists; see http://www.telegraph.co.uk/news/religion/5674934/Richard-Dawkins-launches-childrens-summer-camp-for-atheists.html.

taking sides or expressing what may be interpreted as a "party line" scripted by his Christian father.

Ultimately, I am trying to ask them: What if there is a rational world which does not mock our deepest intuitions and gut-level hunches and dreams? Compared to the barren universe of reductionist modernism, what if there is a larger universe, much more intellectually true and satisfying to reason and at the same time fulfilling the numinous and emotional and symbolic and deeply emotional needs we seem to have and can barely explain without knowing ourselves in the light of God as holistic mind-soul-bodies in God's image? Instead of a small world that drains our deepest selves of legitimacy, this would be a bigger, more compelling, wonder-full universe because it belongs to God. Since wonder, consciousness, intuition, and even love are at the center of our identity and our search for meaning, only an explanation that is unbounded and personal can really work. This is the central vision of *Big Questions*, and of course what its title tries to encapsulate.

The Balmain Tribe are intellectual and I want to honor and utilize that strength while at the same time speaking to their intuitions and gut feelings that there might be a God actually have a profound compelling rationality to them, a rationality that is more fascinating, more compelling than their conventional rationality (which seems to be a naive application of absorbed cultural secularism and its presuppositions).[10]

## God on the Periphery

How important did our respondents find the issue of the existence of God? More than half (seven out of thirteen) found it peripheral to their individual lives, or not important at all. A significant minority (four out of thirteen) found it a significant issue worthy of thought and exploration, but even they found it nonessential to their daily lives and found many other things equally important. A minority (two of thirteen) found it foundational. For them, it

---

10. Private communication with Pastor Anthony MacPherson contributed ideas to this section.

was the question upon which all else was based, and was pivotal in ordering the direction and purpose of their lives.

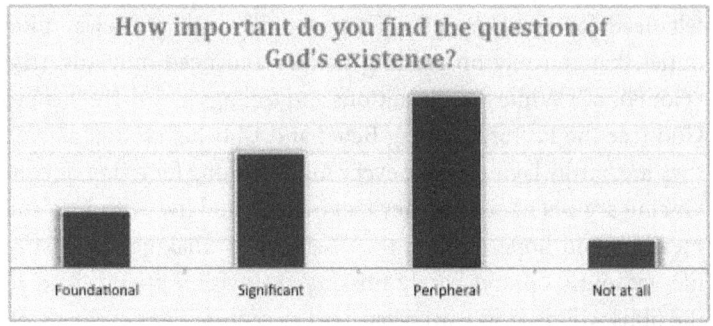

Overall, their assumptions were postmodern in the sense that God could be the Ground of All Being in the Universe or could vanish in a puff of logic[11] depending on the individual's life and sense of relevance. To paraphrase Nietzsche, who gave us a sponge to wipe away the sky? Who told us that all meaning stood or fell on whether or not we perceived it?

Interestingly, most participants say that the importance they have placed on the issue of the existence of God has changed across their lives. Significant life events as well as styles of upbringing were the most common reasons for the shifts. It was evident from the in-depth interviews that a significant number of participants had been brought up with Christian influences (most commonly Sunday school and Christian schooling), but had each had the same experience of reaching a point in their lives where they began to question their Christian roots. It was apparent that at this point they could not find suitable answers, and this then led to a rejection of their religious beliefs as part of their rational adult world. This could then be replaced by a broader notion of spirituality, or by nothing.

---

11. The phrase is from that witty atheist Douglas Adams, *Hitchhiker's Guide to the Galaxy*.

## Asking Big Questions

### Implications

I see two key insights for *Big Questions*.

First, the question of God is not a burning issue or strongly felt need for many people. (Compare this with a freeway food outlet that can rely on existing hunger and need only advertise "Hot Food.") While their intuitions and feelings may drive them to God (see the Factors Driving Belief and Unbelief section above), they are hardly laying awake every night wishing for a sign or convincing argument so that they can believe, and live with love and meaning and hope. Rather, they seem to be making the best of life without God and barely missing an invisible friend. And so the films will need to work very hard to capture their curiosity on various topics which then in turn point to God's existence; that is, the best strategy may be to choose topics that interest them on their own, and show their possible connections with theism. At best, we may tap into some intellectual curiosity and wonder, and move forward using that limited traction.

Second, it would be ideal for our series to find people when they are questioning their beliefs. One could fairly expect them to be more interested and curious and also more motivated to consume media on this topic when they are younger than later in life when they feel they have reached conclusions on the issue of God. The prime stage of questioning seems to be university (though this begins much younger[12]). Hence the strategy that we should target the younger end of the Balmain tribe.

---

12. Hughes, "Characteristics of Religious Knowledge," 146, argues that Australian believers begin questioning faith in primary school. Engebretson, "Young People," 8–19, observes deterioration in attitudes to Christianity after childhood, and explains this by pragmatic career focus and "absorption into the world of work"; family influence; the role of positive personal experience; a need for community; their perception of churches' attitudes on issues of tolerance, for example in how they treat homosexuals; and a postmodern zeitgeist which makes them question all meta-narratives except that of capitalist consumption.

## Life Purpose: Horizontal Only

Regarding the purpose of life, or at least of their lives, the participants were varied in their responses, as the following graph reveals. (Some expressed more than one purpose.)

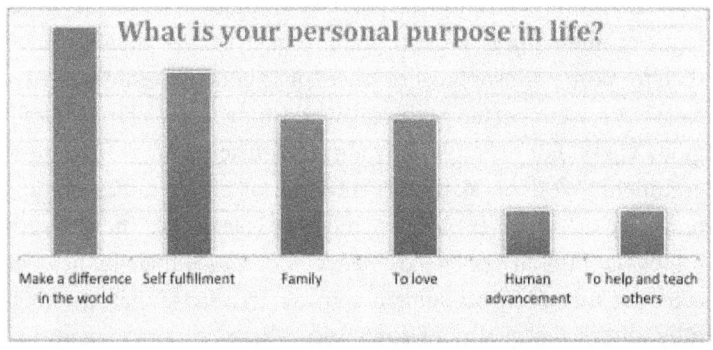

Respondents were conscious of a clear divide between self-centered life purposes and purposes which extended to others and even to broader humanity. More than a third of participants believed that their main life purpose was to make a difference in the world, whether it be for those in their immediate networks (e.g., family and friends) or for the greater community. On the other hand, just under one-third felt that the purpose of life was for self-fulfillment. That is, reasons for living were individual-centric and often guided by their own interest, desires and needs. Quotes in this vein included:

> *I create my own reason for my existence. It could be anything. Right now, it's learning and music...*

> *...People create their own reason to live*

Again, everything is horizontal rather than vertical, self-defined rather than objective.

### Implications

This would suggest that *Big Questions* should speak in real world terms at first, demonstrating the truthfulness of Christianity by observable, real things and also demonstrating the usefulness of Christianity in everyday terms.

Examining our proposed outline of topics in this light, we do focus on the natural world in the first seven films, then when we turn to more philosophical rather than scientific questions, we try to stay very connected with real-world topics in illustrating religious views. For example, episode 7 is a discussion on the moral argument. We look at the urgent issue of child trafficking, and only then ask whether objective morality is possible. Then episode 9 looks at human sexual experience and argues that this may be evidence that a human being is spiritual in a sense that meaningfully affects the quality of supposedly "secular" experiences like this. These are attempts to demonstrate the truth and usefulness of Christianity in very down-to-earth ways.

Of course time will tell how successful this approach is.

## God in My Crisis?

Believers may have traditionally assumed that "there are no atheists in fox-holes," and that crisis can make people turn to God. However the in-depth interviews revealed that for these participants God had almost zero role or relevance—even in a crisis. Rather, the main source of comfort during trials and suffering was external support, with family and friends mentioned as the first source they would reach out to for comfort. The second main source was rationalizing, thinking through the situation, which fits with the intellectualism of the Balmain Tribe. Interviewees often analyzed the context and circumstances in order to gain control and comfort in the midst of crisis or uncertainty.

> *Becoming grounded, instead of running with the emotional side...*

## Qualitative Research and Interpretation

> *I look at the situation and find problems and solutions. I try to use as much reason as possible...*

Their ways of rationalizing included reaffirming the view that things often happened without reason, and trying to live without needing a reason. Other individuals reflected on their own character and concluded that they were a good person.

> *Whatever happens, happens. It doesn't have to happen for a reason...*

> *...Knowing that I'm not a bad person.*

Only a minority relied on faith and, for those who did, it was often at most a prayer to God as a last resort during a crisis.

> *When I am actually scared, it's a natural inclination to ask God...*

## Implications

This would suggest that a personal crisis may not open up many people from the Balmain Tribe to considering faith or God—in fact, they may not even connect personal comfort with the idea of God. The church has traditionally tried to offer support to people in various life crises, and that is of course good for its own sake, but may not prove to be effective as an evangelistic strategy. We may even lose credibility by presenting faith as particularly for times of crisis—and thus, by implication, not for sunny days when my relationships are good and my share portfolio is rising. These responses do suggest that the Balmain Tribe may be open to friendship, which could be an opportunity for a church that is strong on community, but they tend to rely on tried and true relationships. This means church people would need to be in strong relationships well before a crisis. Again, the best approach to the Balmain Tribe seems to be through their intellectual curiosity (assuming, of course, that God will be calling them through the inner witness of the Spirit).

These responses also highlight another major barrier to evangelizing this tribe: the view that "I'm not a bad person," which passes for religious thought. (This matches what I have heard countless times in apologetic speaking.) At a horizontal level alone, it makes sense for a person to compare themselves to others and note that they are not a serial killer or child rapist, and to feel good about that. It makes sense to have positive self-esteem. However, Christian spirituality involves repentance and the notion that one is loved but flawed. (Even from a secular perspective, a realistic self-esteem should into account one's own weak areas.) This should not be misunderstood as reducing a person to a worthless worm, but as recognizing that the human condition involves us being fallen below God's original ideal, and temptible. This is a necessary corollary of the creation story, and is foundational to the gospel Paul preached: he eventually told his audience at Athens to repent (Acts 17:30). He led up to it strategically, building a platform of logic and persuasion, and introduced it after mentioning God's gracious turning of a blind eye; he put it in the polite third person that "all people everywhere" need to repent, but he based it on no less authority than God commanding, and linked it causally to his teaching on final judgment and his teaching about Jesus as judge and resurrected one. It was not long after presenting this idea, linked to a resurrection, that Paul's audience fragmented. Today, one can use similar gracious strategies, and speak of self-examination as vital for healthy personal growth, but eventually Christianity will need to refer the the external authority of God's law and of Jesus as perfectly righteous, and point out my need of forgiveness from the cross and deep change from the spirit, and this can tend to lay the ego in the dust. The gospel, when honestly presented, is still divisive, and I know of no strategy to change that.

*Qualitative Research and Interpretation*

## Reasoning about the Existence of God

During the in-depth interviews, the participants were shown eight written statements arguing for or against the existence of God. These statements (reproduced in the shaded boxes below) were presented in no particular order. Participants were then asked to respond to the arguments, stating whether they agreed or disagreed with each, as well as elaborate on their underlying reasons for their response.

### The Problem of Hell

> *How could a loving God allow people to suffer unending pain for eternity in hell?*

Of all the arguments against the existence of God, this generated the most heartfelt reaction from most participants. They were perplexed as to how a loving God could knowingly allow—or even cause—people to suffer.

> *People suffer enough on earth...*

Even considering those who believed in God at least vaguely, it was evident that most participants did not believe in the traditional concept of hell. Some expressed the belief that hell was a metaphorical concept which did not literally exist. This view was more pronounced in participants who relied more heavily on rational and scientific thinking, and they often deemed the argument irrelevant. That is, for these more rational people, the idea of hell was apparently not a barrier to them engaging with Christianity or the idea of a personal God, but was more like an idea they had dismissed.

> *I believe that whatever is up there, whatever is our greater power, is an all-encompassing, all loving God...there wouldn't be a Hell.*

> *I don't believe in heaven and hell...so I don't see that as an argument as such...*

> *Hell's never been a concept that I've believed existed.*

> *I don't believe in Hell. As I said, I don't really fit into any category on religion. I don't necessarily believe in Heaven either. I don't have any fixed ideas on what happens and where we go when we die. I like to think that it's somewhere nice.*

Interestingly, a few participants noted that while they did not believe in hell, they believed that heaven existed. This could be called wish-fulfilment, or could relate to a more benevolent view of God opposed (in their minds) to a punishing, judgmental God.

> *I don't believe people go to hell. Only the good people go to heaven...*

However, on the other hand, several participants had no difficulty believing in the idea of hell. These participants felt that hell was plausible and indeed necessary for the justice of humanity. They believed that God, if one existed, would have the power, authority and right to allow "bad people" to be punished. Notably, hell was meant for those who were classified as bad people (e.g., murderers, criminals), and nobody mentioned it as a possibility for those in the "ordinary" range rather than extremely sinful. None of these participants seemed to consider the scale of punishment: infinite punishment for finite sin. None mentioned the biblical concept of salvation, grace or Jesus as an exit from condemnation. While these participants were not against the idea of hell per se, they were misinformed about the key surrounding doctrines from Christianity.

> *Where there is good, there is always bad. It's the balance of things. People need to be punished for doing bad things. I believe there is good in everybody, but if there is more bad than good, then they need to be taught a lesson...*

*Qualitative Research and Interpretation*

*I don't think God is asking for too much. I mean, we only have to follow the Ten Commandments, and they're not that unreasonable. If people keep focussing on the negative, then of course people lose faith from it.*

## Implications

This is a genuine challenge. The New Atheists often raise this issue and its implications to malign the justice and kindness of God as traditionally portrayed by Christianity.[13] Recently, this topic has been hotly debated by Christians, particularly evangelicals.[14] Some defend the traditional Christian paradigm of eternal conscious torment.[15] Others argue for universalism.[16] Others argue for temporary hell and then non-existence, or views broadly classified as annihilationism or conditional immortality.[17]

I would not have included this question on the list of arguments for and against, except that Mark McCrindle and Hester Kahei suggested it, partly as a way of balancing the numbers of pros and cons, but also after conducting other Christianity-related research projects. I have often had audiences raise it during question time in outreach meetings, and this research confirms that it is an issue for my target audience. I have considered making a film on

13. For just one example, Dawkins, *God Delusion*, 319–22.

14. McGrath, *Christian Theology*, 458–59, notes that since "the 1980s, a growing internal debate has developed within evangelicalism concerning a network of eschatological issues, centering on the issue of immortality." See also Fudge and Peterson, *Two Views of Hell*; Crockett and Gundry, *Four Views on Hell*.

15. E.g., Carson, *Gagging of God*, 515–36; Harmon, "Case against Conditionalism," 193–224; Gerstner, *Repent or Perish*; Peterson, *Hell on Trial*; Head, "Duration of Divine Judgment"; Packer, "Evangelical Annihilationism"; Packer, "Evangelicals and the Way of Salvation," 107–36.

16. See Parry and Partridge, *Universal Salvation?*; MacDonald, *Evangelical Universalist*; Gulley & Mulholland, *If Grace Is True*.

17. See Edwards and Stott, *Essentials*, 312–20; Green, *Evangelism through the Local Church*, 69ff.; Hughes, *True Image*; Wenham, "Case for Conditional Immortality"; Ellis, "New Testament Teaching"; Fudge, *Fire That Consumes*; Pinnock, "Destruction of the Finally Impenitent."

this topic, interviewing leading Christian thinkers from the three major views so as to suggest a range of possibilities, however I have been surprised at the strength of the reaction to Rob Bell's recent questioning of eternal conscious torment. It seems that touching such an emotive and controversial topic may make churches less likely to use this series. However, if it is a key objection to people finding faith, it does require a good response at some point.

## The Problem of the Supernatural

> *As a rational, scientific modern person I can't believe in a God who deals in angels and demons, resurrections, walking on water and miracles.*

Views were equally split on this argument. It was evident that those participants who were more scientific and evidence-based in their thinking *strongly* agreed with the problem of the supernatural. For them, supernatural elements strongly deterred them from engaging with the idea of God.

> *Yes, I would say that these things make me strongly disagree...*

There were some who somewhat agreed with this argument, and it was noticeable that while their rational minds deterred them from believing that supernatural elements existed, there was also a slight human curiosity in the possibility that angels and demons could perhaps exist. However, overall they felt and indicated that the supernatural was a hard topic for them to digest. Participants often mentioned the view that a belief in particular types of spirit forms (e.g., angels or watching ancestors) depended on social context and culture, based on the assumption that views of the supernatural were traditional, a mere fabrication of culture.

> *Strongly agree. If I was born in America, I would be a Christian. The angel thing is the western notion of an*

## Qualitative Research and Interpretation

*absolute deity of good and evil. Likewise if I was an Indian in America, all their gods have to do with nature.*

*I don't believe in all of those things, like demons and stuff like that, but I do believe in spirits, most from experience knowing people who have seen things. Also, I don't think that everyone completely leaves the earth and doesn't come back.*

A few participants *somewhat* agreed with this argument, though for them this was not a strong issue or the key barrier to faith.

*No, that's not my problem with religion and beliefs... That's not my issue. That's not what is stopping me from believing in it...*

For the other half of interviewees, the supernatural was not an issue at all. Some participants recounted experiences with elements they believed were supernatural and spiritual, while others indicated that they had never had a supernatural experience themselves but had no problem believing that others had and that the supernatural existed.

*I believe in supernatural stuff. I strongly disagree with this argument. There are definitely things out there...*

*There's got to be more than what we can see. I think a lot of what religion does is pushing the realms of what we know to test our faith.*

### Implications

This provides a real challenge.

One could view this as a useful skepticism driven by some of the miraculous claims in popular religion and popular culture, and could agree with it: some things religious people say do deserve to be roundly rejected on the basis of both reason as well as of Scripture. Without here providing an exhaustive definition of what is superstitious and what is genuinely miraculous, a logical rejection of superstition is no threat at all to Christian faith, which does not require the belief that God directly controls every natural phenomenon and is in fact quite compatible with the Creator setting up natural laws to operate in the universe. To win credibility with this audience, it could be important to make clear what biblical Christianity is not saying, and even to distance it from some superstitious beliefs.

Yet I sense that approach would go only so far without being perceived as "spin control," because the answers suggest much more negative views of miraculous claims, for example the resurrection of Jesus. It may be wisest to recognize that skepticism explicitly, and give a two-sided message in response. A one-sided message presents only positive points, but a two-sided message admits the cons but aims to refute them with pros, which is traditionally more credible with a target audience that is educated and has some dissonance on the subject, particularly one that is highly involved in the sense of being very motivated on the issue.[18] (The first two factors definitely apply in this case, although the third one arguably does not.) So a two-sided message would make clear that some religious claims are superstitious and wrong, but adduce rational evidence in support of the resurrection of Jesus, making clear that accepting it as historically true is not agreeing to a Disneyified view that requires miracles every day.

It will also be important to work within the scientific paradigm as much as possible, but to differentiate methodological naturalism (the belief that science functions according to laws without the need for miracles in the equation) from philosophical naturalism (the belief that matter is all there is): even atheists posit a singularity at the beginning of space-time. Taking a scientific approach entails looking for hard evidence on various questions, and giving a fair hearing to nonbelievers but then answering their objections. We have endeavoured to do this in our pilot episode, "The Artificial Albatross," which gives fair voice to Peter Atkins, a leading New Atheist, alongside John Lennox, a Christian. The editorial

18. Craig-Lees et al., *Consumer Behaviour*, 232.

## Qualitative Research and Interpretation

voice of the film is my own, and it declares its biases by introducing me as a Christian, but the film also tries to be fair in terms of allowing both sides of the issue to be thoroughly explored. (It also offers a DVD extra of a debate between both professors, 100 mins. in duration and absolutely uncut to be transparent about possible editorial bias.) This very process is designed to model that we have nothing to fear from discussion and debate, and that the belief we are promoting is not blind faith.

Further, the first six topics of *Big Questions* are scientific, with input from leading scientists on both sides of the God question. Philosophical questions come next, and only at the end of the series, when some scientific evidence suggesting a God has been adduced, do we turn to the miraculous. (I personally believe Creation itself is miraculous, but I am using the word in the sense of miracles.) I believe we have biblical warrant for an apologetical process in this shape. Even Jesus, talking to a great intellectual, started with "earthly things" because speaking of "heavenly things" may have strained his listener's credulity (John 3:12). Paul recognized the need of a phased strategy, starting with what is more acceptable (e.g., 1 Cor 3:2) and, as discussed above, began with what was known to the Athenians and left the issue of resurrection till last. We will begin with nature, and various arguments for theism based on it.

Later in the series, of course, we do discuss the "miracle" of Christ's resurrection. We will make clear at this point that it is impossible to find scientific evidence on historical questions: with resurrection we are in the domain of legal-historical proof rather than the scientific of observability and repeatability. Hopefully by then, however, we have given enough evidence to suggest that God exists, and if that is established, then believing in God's occasional activity is not such a long stretch. We will do so in the paradigm of many Christian thinkers[19] who have dealt with miracles as part of

---

19. See, e.g., Craig, *Reasonable Faith*, chap. 6, "The Problem of Miracles"; Geivett and Habermas, *In Defense of Miracles*; Earman, "Bayes, Hume and Miracles"; Earman, *Hume's Abject Failure*; Hesse, "Miracles and the Laws of Nature"; Swinburne, *Concept of Miracle*; Swinburne, *Miracles*.

## Asking Big Questions

a rational (as opposed to rationalist) worldview, explaining them as temporary suspensions of natural law.

In the face of skepticism of this sort, it will be important to offer extraordinary evidence for the extraordinary claim that Jesus rose from the dead, as we will see below. It will not be enough to assume that belief either comes or does not come after simply hearing the gospel of the resurrection.

## The Problem of Pain

> *The fact that people suffer suggests there cannot be a God who is wise, kind and strong enough to stop it.*

A majority of interviewees were inclined to disagree with this argument. Of those who disagreed, there was a general feeling that if God existed, suffering and pain in the world would not be his responsibility. Further, just under half *strongly* disagreed, and so participants seemed to acknowledge that the freedom of living in the world was accompanied with the potential of pain and suffering, and they did not hold attribute this to God. Some expressed the view that pain and suffering were often necessary in life, for learning and endurance.

> *Everyone is responsible. It's not God's fault what happens to us. We have freedom.*

> *I personally believe everything happens for a reason. But I'm not going to lie, I don't know what the reason is. I agree that bad things happen, but I wouldn't agree that because they do, God doesn't exist.*

> *The best lessons in life are hard. Pain is because of the world's problems…*

> *I think that humans cause a lot of the pain and it's not God's place to step in. I think the humans need to solve their own problems. If we cause it, we need to fix it.*

## Qualitative Research and Interpretation

At most, only a minority of participants somewhat agreed with this argument. Those who *somewhat* agreed argument tended to be those who had stronger opinions against Christianity and were not themselves spiritual at all. These people felt that if God existed, he would be merciful and suffering would not be evident in the world. These feelings were magnified when it came to issues such as suffering that they perceived as unjust, such as global calamities and natural disasters, as well as the death of a loved one.

> *If God is merciful, then people wouldn't suffer...*

> *I would somewhat agree with that. How can God let children suffer...?*

> *Sometimes I see things that happen to people and I wonder, why them?*

> *I saw a religious guy who said, they must have sinned. They sinned therefore they must have deserved it, which is ridiculous because a child born in Africa certainly has not sinned.*

Some did not naturally connect suffering with the idea of God at all, but just saw it as part of the world as it is, almost as if "Why?" questions about the provenance or ontological status of suffering would be pointless to direct to an empty sky.

> *A lot of people just take everything as it comes and deal with it when it happens. They don't think about God, they just want to deal with it and move on. Other people don't believe in a God anymore because (they don't understand) how it can happen...*

### Implications

I was surprised that this was not much more of an issue. Audiences raise the issue of suffering almost immediately, and people's responses suggest they feel it deeply, whether they are believers in God or not.

This may be partly explained by the way I have framed the question. I phrased it objectively in terms that some apologists call the logical problem of evil in the world. I could have phrased it more subjectively, in terms of my personal suffering and God's non-response, in line with what some apologists call the experiential problem of evil. I find this a tougher question. To my mind, Plantinga's Christian Free Will Defense offers the beginnings of a satisfying answer to the problem of evil. Yet the experiential problem is much harder to answer: if God is all-knowing, all-loving, and all-powerful, then why did God not choose to prevent my suffering or that of the person I love? I find this much more complex, emotionally and intellectually. It could be that our participants have thought through the logical problem of evil fairly readily and so did not think it fair to blame God (if there is one) when human free choice accounts for so much. I thought of phrasing the statement more personally (e.g., the fact that I suffer…), but that could spill over into experiential arguments for God, and I wanted to keep this section more objective.

This research would seem to suggest that the Christian Free Will Defense would make sense to this audience, and may be reinforcing what they already believe. If handled right, this answer could produce strong agreement, yet it may be telling people what they already know, and may prove to be an answer to a question they are not particularly asking.

This result could also perhaps be explained by participants being so used to a world with evil and suffering in it that they could not seriously think of a world without this, seeing that as a construct of children and superstitious religion. Some participants at least could not seem to imagine personal growth and development without it. This highlights the point that Christian notions of perfect after-life in heaven or a new Earth are radically difficult for people to believe, requiring a major rethink of ecology, social relations, the body and everything. When God says, "I am making all

*Qualitative Research and Interpretation*

things new" and speaks of a world with "no more tears or suffering or pain" (Revelation 21:4–5), this is a major statement.

## Sexual Behavior

> *Religious rules about sexual behaviour are old-fashioned and repressive, and they seem to make people feel guilty for no reason. If God exists and is loving, then why does God's law seem so judgmental?*

Only a small minority agreed with this argument, while the overwhelming majority disagreed to some extent. Interestingly, this was not seen as an argument which deterred participants from believing in God. Regardless of whether participants agreed or disagreed with religious rules (i.e., on sexual behaviour), it was notably irrelevant to belief or otherwise in God's existence.

> *For me, that wouldn't change anything.*

> *I don't ascribe [sic] to any belief system, not because of its limiting rules. That to me misses the forest for the trees. So supposing that there exists a religion that all I have to do is believe in God, but I'm allowed to have affairs, be bisexual, do it with who I want and where I want and, heck, even get paid to do these things, I still wouldn't do it...*

Those who disagreed with the statement were very varied on the question of belief in God. Generally, however, those who did not believe in God and did not agree with this argument said they did not feel it related to their overall decision regarding God's existence.

> *I think it is a bit outdated, but I respect people who do follow that. I think in this generation it is now more acceptable to go with either choice.*

Generally, too, those who were more open to the idea of God existing were more understanding of religious rules regarding sexual behaviour and even tolerant of them, however this did not necessarily mean that they personally followed these rules.

> I don't think God is judgmental. I'd say yes, those morals are quite old-fashioned, sex before marriage and homophobia for example, but I wouldn't say that He's being judgmental in having those standards.

> I think that God is trying to influence us to believe the things He believes...

## Implications

I find these results surprisingly positive and I am not sure that the question as I wrote it really uncovered the areas I thought it would, or elicited responses relevant to my question.

This research seems to suggest sexuality is an outlier for our participants rather than a key issue. However this puzzles me because of the frequency with which people have raised with me the issue of sex as a barrier to them following God. This is especially true on questions of homosexuality, and even people who are heterosexual themselves will suggest Christianity is threatening a basic human right of gay people to be accepted. I have also found people often raise the dark issue of clergy sexual abuse of children. This has certainly been used as a weapon in the culture wars, for example by the Eros Foundation, the peak body of the pornography industry in Australia, who have publicized reports of clergy abuse, aiming, among other things, to "show the effects of celibacy and sexual repression in the faces of those who extol its virtues."[20] (In fairness, not all the clergy they list are from churches that advocate clerical celibacy.) The church has often been blamed for this issue and for mishandling and denial of it—Australian human rights lawyer Geoffrey Roberston has highlighted this as a serious legal issue.[21] Christianity is often faulted for a dark view of

20. See, e.g., Eros Foundation, *Hypocrites*.
21. Robertson, *Case of the Pope*.

## Qualitative Research and Interpretation

the body and of sexuality or, as atheist philosopher Michel Onfray puts it,

> hatred of the corruptible body, disparaged in every aspect, while the soul—eternal, immortal, divine—is invested with all the higher qualities...; and finally hatred of women...[and their replacement by] the Angel, a bloodless archetype, in preference to real women.[22]

So many would see Christianity as hopelessly hypocritical on this topic, theoretically anti-pleasure but in fact unable to stop even its leaders from behaving in ways that contravene one of the greatest commandments of secular culture: child protection. I intended for this question to raise these questions, and to elicit responses that mapped perceptions of these problems.

On reflection, it could be that one factor to help explain these results is that notions of spirituality and God's existence have been so disconnected from the human institutions of religion (the mainstream church) and their failings and hypocrisies and rules. If that is true, then it would be strategic not to raise these questions in a film series on the existence of God. However, this issue comes up so often in public questions from secular people that I am led to consider whether this research may need much more detail and nuance. It may be that this question relates not to people's views on God's actual existence, but to their consideration of what type of God may exist and whether that God is good and loveable from their perspective; that is, the question fits less in level 1 than in level 2 of the pyramid (see the *Big Questions*: A Brief History section in chap. 1). If that is right, then it would be important to raise the question and offer a Christian response, but not too early in the apologetic process or too early in this film series. I still plan to do this, though frankly this decision is based on personal experience and intuition, as well as overwhelming support from anyone in ministry with whom I have discussed this, rather than the research described above. The research is just one question, a few minutes in the interview process, which is fairly slim data and I need to

---

22. Onfray, *Atheist Manifesto*, 63.

be tentative. I plan to research this topic particularly, ideally in a series of in-depth interviews devoted to issues of sexuality from an apologetic perspective. It could ask people about their views of sexual morality, their views of Christian sexual morality and love. It could ask how much the clergy abuse scandal is hurting the image of Christianity: is it perceived as just a few bad apples acting in an un-Christian way, or is it seen as a contradiction at the heart of core Christianity? I know of no research like this. I feel it would be necessary before I spend an entire film budget on the issue.

## Arguments For the Existence of God

### The Argument from Consciousness

> *The human mind is more than the physical brain, and cannot be explained as a product of a universe that has only matter and no mind elsewhere in it or behind it. A better explanation would be a larger Mind, i.e., God, giving us consciousness.*

Of all the arguments for the existence of God, the argument from consciousness engaged participants the most. That is, this was found to be one of the strongest arguments for the existence of God. An overwhelming majority agreed with this point, and it was notable that this agreement was robust. In addition, of those who agreed, almost all *strongly agreed* with this point.

> *I strongly agree. God did this.*

Further, of the minority that disagreed, only one stated a *strong* disagreement with this specific argument. This argument resonated with those who classified themselves as non-spiritual and were more rational in their thinking. While several attempted to justify their disagreement with evolutionary theory and other scientific arguments, it was evident that they had no deeply considered argument themselves; they had homespun assumptions based on evolution, but no solid rebuttal of this argument. Through the interviews, it was clear that this argument generated interest and discussion from this group.

> *I somewhat disagree. Evolution developed the mind over time...*

> *That's the ultimate question I have trouble answering... the whole notion of consciousness is something that comes alive...in humans...*

> *We're not the only things with minds. Our intelligence is greater than animals but animals also have personalities... so I don't think that is necessarily true.*

> *Animals have brains and personalities and intelligence... So, I don't think that's entirely true.*

## Implications

This seems to be a topic of high interest and also of high potential agreement with Christianity. This is most encouraging, and I intend to develop an entire episode fairly early in the series on this topic. I will seek an interview with J. P. Moreland and perhaps Richard Swinburne, who have treated this topic[23] from a Christian perspective, and as counterpoint making the nay case, with Daniel Dennett, a philosopher of mind and director of the Center for Cognitive Studies at Tufts University, as well as a prominent New Atheist with a large publishing and media profile. I may also interview with Steven Conifer[24] or someone who can present similar specific arguments. My own scripting will borrow from the creative approach of Robert Adams.[25]

The advantage in presenting this argument, at least on my experience with live audiences, is that people sense it intuitively.

---

23. Moreland, "Argument from Consciousness"; Swinburne, "Arguments from Consciousness."

24. Conifer, "Argument from Consciousness Refuted."

25. Adams, "Flavors, Colors and God."

## Asking Big Questions

While some people immediately think of evolution as the solution, this argument is not even close to fleshed out. The argument from consciousness can be presented at a popular level or can also go quite deep philosophically. It does not constitute knockdown proof, and issues of philosophy of mind seem fairly subjective and constructed at a more advanced level, but I have seen audiences find it quite persuasive.

### The Cosmological Argument

> *The universe could not have kick-started itself, so there must be something outside it.*

Over half of all participants agreed with this argument and it was evident that it engaged with them intellectually and philosophically. Interestingly, almost all who agreed felt *strongly* about this argument. Although participants were not able to explain reasons for their agreement, it was because of this (i.e., lack of other plausible explanations) which seemed to propel and incline them toward believing that God could exist as a results of this argument.

> *You can't explain those things. The creation of mankind and you think "Oh God is so smart!" I think most people do believe that there is something out there that created it all…*
>
> *I strongly agree. Sciences are trying to prove everything happened as a reaction…*

Interestingly, for a small number of participants, the combination of both science and a possible creator was plausible.

> *There's also a lot of science that shows exactly how it happened. That doesn't mean that the two of them can't somehow mix together somewhere. I think that somewhere they cross over if you go back far enough.*

Those who disagreed with this argument based their decision on being "rational" and "logical." For these participants, their decision was strongly swayed by their belief in science and rational knowledge. Although they themselves were not able to explain or justify the scientific theories which underlay their stances, their belief in the ability of science to explain everything, was unshakeable.

> *Strongly disagree. My beliefs and knowledge. I will look at from the information about how the world came into being, rather than God making it happen.*

For others who disagreed with the cosmological argument, it was apparent that this argument elicited philosophical thinking and discussion. For these participants, this argument was not enough prove the existence of God. Rather, it was seen as a never-ending question with no clear answer. Furthermore, these participants felt that others, who claimed to have answers to the argument, did so on a basis of their own contextual beliefs and understanding rather than rational, logical knowledge.

> *If there is something outside or someone who created the Big Bang...then who created that someone? You just keep going backwards...*

> *No one knows. No one can prove God exists or the big bang happened...*

> *From a philosophical point of view, I can ask a spiritual person where they think the world came from...(the never ending question).*

## Implications

This argument seemed to promote agreement with more than half of our participants. While this is not quantitative research, the deep feeling with which many agreed suggest that this area is both interesting and persuasive to many.

## Asking Big Questions

For some participants, this topic accesses the view that science and God are not incompatible. This is a key idea we are trying to promote, both explicitly at times and implicitly in every episode, and it will be important here to respect science and its current views and utilize them in making a case suggesting God. Some Christians and Jews welcome Big Bang theory as being quite compatible with the biblical account because it posits a beginning to space-time—and a singularity at that.[26] Others find that incompatible with Scripture, or question the science.[27] Again, for reasons of unity and pragmatism, we will avoid raising that contentious issue. We will look instead at the results rather than the method.

Some participants in our interviews seemed to revert to the default position that science can explain everything, a common assumption in Western culture. So this topic may offer some opportunity to make entering wedge arguments, and to promote a philosophy of science and religion as being compatible rather than adversarial, however this will not work for everybody.

Some participants are happy to admit that this area is a mystery to them, and may look down on those who confidently claim to have the answers, considering them simplistic and insufficiently broad. It is important to take this as a caveat to unjustifiable certainty. We do not know exactly what happened, and we will win credibility by asking pointed questions but not claiming total answers.

---

26. Schroeder, *Genesis and the Big Bang*.

27. John Hartnett is a research professor at the University of Western Australia. See Hartnett, *Starlight, Time and the New Physics*; Williams and Hartnett, *Dismantling the Big Bang*.

## Design and Fine-Tuning Arguments

### The Design Argument

> The existence of superb engineering in nature (e.g., a bird's flying technologies) suggests an Engineer. The incredible language-like complexity and "spelling" of DNA (3.5 billion chemical letters, compared to 130,000 for Hamlet) suggests an Author.

### The Fine Tuning Argument

> The fact that so many factors went right for planet Earth to support human life, plus that so many physics variables are at just the right settings for the universe to exist, suggests a God.

Just under half of participants agreed with this argument, and these all expressed that they *strongly* agreed. It was evident that those who agreed felt that this was a strong argument directly related to the existence of God. However, there was also a direct correlation between those who stated agreement with the argument, and a reliance on feelings over rationality when it came to the existence of God. More specifically, those who had previously communicated that they placed a stronger emphasis on feelings and intuitions over the rational, logical and scientific, were also those who stated a strong agreement with the design argument.

> *I actually think that there must be a God for all this to happen in the world...*

Interestingly, a couple of participants swiftly dismissed this argument even though they held different views on the existence of God. For these participants, the coexistence of spirituality and science was unfeasible and implausible. That is, for this cohort, it seemed strange to talk about God through the medium of science.

> *It seems ironic that we need science to prove religion.*

## Asking Big Questions

When it came to the design arguments, those who disagreed with this argument felt strongly about it, basing their claims and beliefs heavily on evolution. It was interesting to note that even though these participants themselves were unable to explain or justify their evolutionary standpoint, they clung to evolutionary theory with a resilient conviction and confidence.

> *There's so much research to discuss evolution and how we've come to this perfection...*

> *One person could not create so many things. It must be other factors.*

> *I actually tend to think that the complexity and grandness suggests no God.*

> *If there is a God, then where did he come from?*

> *I strongly disagree—it the same beauty both a spiritual or non-spiritual person sees. But it's their ideas and beliefs that make them choose particular side...*

Interestingly, for a couple of participants, both sides of the argument seemed plausible. It was evident that while these participants believed in the role of science and evolution, there was still a possibility for something else (i.e., God) to be behind it all.

> *I do believe in the science of things and I do believe that there's been lots of trial and error along the way, that these things didn't just happen overnight. Like the evolution of man, I believe that we did come from monkeys...I look at incredible architecture that we have and things that humans have built, and I think even then, what gave humans, these architects and engineers, these ideas? I don't necessarily think that is just evolution...I think that is something greater.*

*Qualitative Research and Interpretation*

## Implications

This issue appears to be something of a battleground, with people already carrying strong convictions either way. It seems especially hard to make the design argument on biological topics, because evolution seems to be the totalizing explanation that owns popular perceptions of scientific logic, while notions of divine creation are held more emotionally. Further, the classic theistic argument from design is often popularly equated with the Intelligent Design movement, which can be associated politically with George W. Bush as a means of ridiculing it, for example by ABC science journalist Robyn Williams.[28]

In retrospect, I sense I should have researched the fine-tuning argument separately from the design argument. While they are related, I have noticed in live presentations that discussing the stars and the origin of the universe rises above the "Darwin wars" of biology, which have been endlessly fought: Dawkins himself is constantly arguing against any notion of creation. Yet I know of no cosmologist who seriously suggests that stars and planets have evolved in a biological sense of mutating and reproducing and being selected for greater survivability. The term "evolution" is often used of the life cycle of a star and, however different this process is from the biological, it seems to access the paradigm and the popular assumptions that it can explain everything. To a non-scientist, this can seem unarguable.

Those who are convinced the evolution alone can explain all life and apparent design hold this view in spite of gaps, feeling confident that science will eventually explain the gaps. To be fair, it seems like a choice between God of the gaps or science of the gaps. It could be a strategic move to get them to question whether science can explain everything, but not in a way that sounds anti-science: Christianity already suffers from misperceptions on that score. It seems to me that once again the logical communication strategy is to feature top-level scientists who are also believers,

---

28. Williams, *Unintelligent Design*.

## Asking Big Questions

making the point that science and religion can coexist happily, and also giving people independent evidence to consider.

### The Moral Argument

> *There are moral absolutes. (E.g., It is never morally right to rape. It is never right to cause unnecessary pain to a child or an animal.) But we cannot get moral absolutes from nature (because the jungle is about survival of the fittest and my "selfish genes," not altruism or loving my neighbor). We can get some morals from society, but these change with times and places (e.g., in 1930s Germany, racism seemed OK). Historically, the only place humans have found moral absolutes is in the idea of a God who holds me accountable for how I treat my neighbour and cares about everyone.*

> *So the existence of morality suggests that God exists.*

More than half of the participants agreed with this argument, claiming that human morals were based on God or on Christian values.

> *I think that it's inbuilt in us that it's wrong to cause harm to anyone. God's responsible for that...*

However, it was notable that for some who agreed, agreement was based on their perceptions of Christian morality, rather than on God as ultimate judge and moral creator. Notably, many of those whom agreed with this argument based their decision on their belief that morals are founded from biblical laws such as the Ten Commandments, rather than reflecting on the source of those morals (i.e., God the creator).

> *I agree with that to a degree. But then I also think your reactions to things are based on how you are brought up. But that comes back to religion anyhow.*

## Qualitative Research and Interpretation

> *I do agree. I think it all goes back to the Bible and the Ten Commandments, and everything has evolved like that. We've built social constructs of these traditions.*

One participant acknowledged that morals were contextual, but still thought that a higher power was the source of morality.

> *I would say that a lot of those moral rules, if you like, are still created by humans, of what is acceptable and what is not...I think at some level, people always [know] what [is] right...I think a lot of it is instinct, and then instinct comes from a higher power...I think if you tracked it far enough back, I would put that down to a higher power.*

All of those who disagreed with the moral argument felt *strongly* about their disagreement. They were unable to attribute morality to a God, stating that morality was a human construct which was contextual but also innate. These participants felt that it was wrong, and even offensive, to claim that morality was independent of humans and to claim that we needed a God construct in order to be good. Foundational to this view was the belief that morality was shaped and influenced by society and the environment. That is, they were social constructivists rather than objectivists. They had no problem at all with the notion that morality was a very fluid and malleable construct.

> *I strongly disagree with moral absolutism. Morality is something that changes with time...My understanding of science says otherwise. Many species, later on down the line, altruism does come out.*

> *People have their own personal accountability. They have a conscience. I don't have to answer to a God to know that I shouldn't kill someone. I don't believe God is who holds me accountable.*

> *Morality is a human thing. We have laws and ethics we live by and they're human constructs.*

## Asking Big Questions

> *I think morals are constantly changing. I think eventually not only will societal morals have changed, but also Biblical ones.*
>
> *I think these would have been developed over time with society.*

### *Implications*

It may sound pessimistic to say that those who disagreed with this argument seemed generally to understand it better than those who thought they agreed. With one exception, those who agreed mistook it for a historical claim that society's morals came historically from Judaeo-Christian sources. While this is arguably partly true, at least in the West, and tangentially relevant, it misses the point of the moral argument, which is an argument for theism generally rather than necessarily being an argument for Christian theism in particular.[29] This occurred probably because our statement needed to be so brief, and could not fully outline what the moral argument says and what it does not say. It could be argued that we have not really researched the moral argument itself, and in retrospect we should perhaps have given a one-page statement with more detail. And yet we have discovered some common ways in which the moral argument can be misheard, and that this is useful in shaping our approach.

Those who disagreed seemed closer to understanding the point, though some seemed to think the point was that one could not be good without God. I have noticed in live audiences a tendency to misunderstand this point, and so I always try to state very clearly that I have non-theistic friends who live moral lives and, as a believer myself, sometimes fall below my moral code. Professor John Lennox acknowledges this in the bonus interviews on the DVD of the pilot episode. I believe this is a common biblical theme, evidenced in "righteous Gentiles" like Rahab, Naaman and others,

---

29. For definitions, see, e.g., Byrne, "Moral Arguments"; Adams "Moral Arguments."

## Qualitative Research and Interpretation

referred to by Jesus (Luke 4:24-29; 10:10-15), and argued by Paul: "Gentiles who have not the law" can be "a law unto themselves," showing the law is written on their hearts (Rom 2:12-14), yet Paul still calls for repentance from his Gentile audience in Athens. I do believe in personal accountability and a moral sense that is innate in secular people. Further, it is true that morals change over time: witness the slavery and racism in Christian history. These points ought to be acknowledged at the outset so that they do not distract from what the moral argument is. I will need to keep this in mind in scripting and editing this episode.

Some have recently argued that morals can be determined from evolutionary science[30] and yet solid responses exist on this point.[31]

Importantly, many who disagreed with the moral argument based this on the belief that morality is socially constructed. I believe this is best countered by arguing a polite reductio ad absurdum using extreme examples. For example, would it ever be morally right for a man to rape a woman? To torture a child or an animal needlessly? To discriminate against a person on the basis of race? Someone who answers no is acknowledging that there are some moral absolutes, and that is enough to undermine constructivism. Someone who answers yes goes against very widely held social standards. I have often used this wedge argument in presenting and debating for Christianity. I once had a student see where the argument was going and try to get off the horns of the dilemma by saying, "I can't judge. I can't say whether it would be right or wrong for someone else to rape under some circumstances." I did not

---

30. Harris, *Moral Landscape*; Nowak, *Super Cooperators*.

31. E.g., see Byrne, "Moral"; Adams, "Moral Arguments"; Adams "Prospects for a Metaethical Argument," 315; Adams *Finite and Infinite Goods;* Alston "Response to Zagzebski"; Wrainwright, *Religion and Morality*, 116; Hare, *Moral Gap*; Hare, *Why Bother Being Good?*; Layman, "God and the Moral Order"; Layman, "God and the Moral Order"; Layman, "Moral Argument"; Hare, *Moral Faith and Providence*; Hare, "Is Moral Goodness without Belief in God Morally Stable," in Garcia and Kind, *Is Goodness without God*, 85; Layman, "God and the Moral Order"; Layman, "God and the Moral Order: Replies," 309. Linville, "Moral Argument"; Street "Darwinian Dilemma," 119.

## Asking Big Questions

need to say anything, as there was a barrage of moral outrage from the largely secular audience. His argument was internally consistent and, apparently to the audience, build on a wrong foundation.

A strong historical case can be made that morality, at least as most secular people experience it, is socially constructed. However, one counter is that socially constructed morality gave us the Tasmanian Aboriginal near-genocide approved by Charles Darwin,[32] and Dachau, and Stalinist purges, and the killing fields of Cambodia.

Here one can deploy standard arguments against relativism.[33]

## Attitudes to Christians: Word Association

Participants were given a word and asked to provide other words which they automatically associate with it. Results are illustrated graphically below, where font size roughly corresponds to frequency of mention or depth of feeling, without trying to claim the clarity of large quantitative research here. (Colors or shadings are merely to enhance readability, rather than having any emphasis.)

### People Who Believe in God

---

32. Darwin, *Voyage of the Beagle*, 424, 430.
33. See, e.g., Beckwith and Koukl, *Relativism*.

*Qualitative Research and Interpretation*

Perceptions of people who believe in God were varied, however it was notable that associations were positively skewed, with more affirmative keywords apparent. When thinking of people who believed in God, participants most commonly perceived them as good, religious, and spiritual people.

## People Who Practice Religion

When it came to people who more specifically practiced a religion, responses were also varied. However, there was a clear divide in characteristics which participants associated with this group. While some notably highlighted the objective, structured and obligatory "doing" aspects of religion, others noted the more spiritual aspects such as faith, journey and devotion.

## Christians Who Regularly Attend Church

Zooming in more precisely on Christians who regularly attend church, perceptions were notably skewed positively, with a majority expressing a general sense of admiration for the dedication they perceived in such Christians. Key words most commonly expressed were "good" and "dedicated."

## Followers of Jesus

Interestingly, when concentrating on "followers of Jesus," the most commonly associated characteristics were that they were Christian and good.

> Having a bit of faith at the back of mind gives you a bit of comfort. I have a lot of religious friends, and they just seem nicer, *a little* gentler, *a little more* accepting.
>
> They're very good at understanding *people, they're* not judgmental. *They're* accepting, *and they're* kind-hearted.

However, it was noticeable that other perceptions were not as positive, with a noticeable sense that followers of Jesus were judgemental, fanatical and akin to "blind sheep."

## Born-Again Christians

**Annoying**

Kind  ReligiousScary
Sincere **Passionate**  Segregation Repentance
**Found good**  Strays return
over the top
misguided  **Extreme**
Confused **Intense** Fanatic
Christian

As the word associations delved into the labels so often utilized self-referentially in the Christian community, perceptions were noticeably more negative. The term "born-again Christian" was seen as significantly different to a "normal" Christian. While a minority had positive perceptions, and indicated that born-again Christians were kind, sincere and good, a majority commonly stated strongly that they were annoying. There was also a general consensus that born-again Christians were confused and notably more extreme than the "average kind-hearted Christian."

## Evangelical Christians

Deluded
Religious Enthusiastic
Convert people   Wrong   Judgmental
Very non-secular
Televangelists        over the top
Unsure Obsessive Excluding   Fanatic
Radical

It was clear that participants felt strongly negative about this "type" of Christian. To them, the evangelical Christian often resulted in a sense of radical fanaticism, often typified by extreme televangelists. Participants felt that evangelists were over the top and enthusiastically deluded.

## Perceptions of Christians

When exploring what participants thought of most Australians' views of Christians generally, there was an especially diverse range of responses, broadly categorized under three headings: Against, Strongly Against, and Accepting. There was a sense that most respondents considered Australians generally to be against Christians, naming doubt, sensitivity and judgment as the reasons for the phenomenon.

> People are weirded out by Christians. They immediately think of Hillsong.

> People find Christians imposing.

> Australians are dubious of Christianity and so they treat Christians as outsiders.

> *It's so easy to offend people these days. So many people seem to be just against religion.*
>
> *Preachers and believers are looked down on.*

However, within this category, some respondents defended their own views against public Christianity even while acknowledging that the trend existed.

> *Faith should be kept inside your heart. As an Arab viewing Australian Christians, I wish religion was less secular and kept out of politics and decisions that affect the livelihood of everyday Australians.*

Some took this view further, saying they found most Australians to be strongly against Christianity. This group tended to offer less justification for the current zeitgeist, explaining the common view in a more apologetic way.

> *A lot of atheists tend to hate Christians.*
>
> *Atheists are actually quite "bible-bashing."*

Finally, a third group opted for the opposing view, not seeing any issue of negative perceptions among average Australians toward Christians. While not undermining the tenability of this viewpoint generally, it ought to be noted that several of these views were proffered by the same respondents within the group who had in previous questions considered Christians to be "obsessive," "fanatical," and "annoying."

> *I don't think we're that cynical.*
>
> *On the whole, people view Christians positively.*
>
> *People are very accepting of other beliefs, particularly of Christianity.*

Asking Big Questions

## Views of Non-Christians

Respondents were then asked to think of the keywords that first sprung to mind when they thought of non-Christians. These automatic responses were largely in keeping with the views the respondents had already made clear on Christians and Christianity generally, and can be neatly divided into two broad groups, positive and negative. Those who held positive views of non-Christians associated them with words such as:

> *Scientific, reasonable, respectable, logical, having the capacity to reason, learned, mathematical, evolutionary.*

Conversely, those who held disparaging views of non-Christians associated them with words such as:

> *Arrogant, lost, weak, scared, discontent, bitter, proud, broken, stubborn, detached, defensive, ignorant, narrow-minded, belligerent.*

Respondents here seemed to associate being non-Christian with being non-religious at all, rather than thinking of non-Christians religions. This may be to do with the context of the questionnaire, which framed the questions in terms of Christianity.

Some of these respondents went beyond the bounds of the question and offered explanations for their views, justifying their disapproval of non-Christians with reference to their complacency.

> *They haven't studied it enough. It's just an easy option.*

One particular respondent stood out from the group, being the only one to convincingly reconcile a positive and negative perspective of non-Christians in the one view:

> *Non-Christians are highly intelligent but morally distraught.*

## Implications

These results have some obvious applications. Though I regard myself as evangelical and born again, I would not choose those terms with this audience. Terms like "Christian" and "follower of Jesus" seem to have had the best response and least baggage.

I also found the comparison of Christians and non-Christians quite instructive. The results seem clearly reflective of two different attitudes—for example, some call non-Christians narrow-minded and ignorant, while most see them as owning the rational/intellectual space (which matches our previous finding). However, some participants highlighted the contrasting perceptions of non-Christians: rational but broken. If this is reflective of the perception of non-Christian people—and further research would have to be done to clarify this—then this may be an opportunity to speak to felt needs.

## Do Beliefs Have an Effect on the Way People Live?

Respondents were asked if they thought that having beliefs changed the way that people lived. Most respondents firmly believed that it did, arguing that true religion necessarily involved a change in lifestyle:

> *Definitely. If you're a Christian you need to do things like pray and read the Bible, whereas nonbelievers can do whatever they please.*

> *Yes, they will live their life according to their belief. Those who don't believe live their life with different belief systems.*

> *Yes, but it depends on what you believe. Some people become very loving and forgiving. Religions give them a conscience and accountability. Others no. It depends on your interpretation.*

Others who held this same view justified it on different grounds, relying less on the necessary outworking of belief systems on lifestyles and more on the lack of guiding principles for those who do not have a belief system:

> *Yes people who don't believe are reckless, they have no direction, no purpose, and no guidance.*

> *To certain people yes, there's people who without Christianity would be lost. I think it's a good set of rules and morals to live by.*

> *Yes. It gives you a purpose.*

There were some respondents who indicated that while having a belief system indeed changed the way people lived, this fact needed to be qualified in some way, such as which specific areas of your life religion would affect, or whether this status quo was desirable or not.

> *Yes. Not in your day-to-day life, but in your overall outlook. Having a spiritual side is a great comfort.*

> *It can make a difference, but it shouldn't in particular.*

Finally, there were those who did not think that belief had any effect on the way people lived. These responses tended to follow two main schools of thoughts, justifying their views either on the basis of cultural relativity, or of strong opinions that morality is a variable independent of religion:

> *In Australia no, but in other countries, definitely.*

> *No, I believe you can still be good and moral without a belief system.*

> *I don't think it does, nor should it. It's a personal thing.*

## Implications

This question was encouraging in that a number of participants thought real religion does change a life, rather than seeing it as hypocritical. The minority view that there was little connection between religion and behaviour seems like more "push-back" against the moral argument, as popularly mutated. It probably relates to views of perceived Christian judgmentalism and moral superiority and is an attempt to hit back at that.

# Jesus

When asked to give their views specifically on the person of Jesus Christ, the broad consensus among respondents was positive, with not a single unequivocally negative comment being made about the man. Comments ranged from the generic:

> *He was a carpenter.*
>
> *He was caring.*
>
> *He was a great story-teller. I like many of his quotes.*

Some comments were notably more developed and well thought out.

> *Christians should be more Christ-like instead of Christian. They should fall away from ideology, but follow Christ.*
>
> *He was God's son, he died for our sins, and he was perfect.*
>
> *He had the perfect example of a good life.*

Several of the respondents balanced their skepticism toward biblical validity and credibility with their admiration of Jesus, differentiating between the two with occasional poignancy:

> *I think he was a real man, but over time the stories have been changed. It's like Chinese whispers.*

## Asking Big Questions

> I think that if he was a real person, he was a great person. He did things regardless of how people viewed him, and he especially gave to people who had nothing.

> Religion forms after someone very heroic or admirable dies.

## Jesus: Real, Divine, the Son of God?

Respondents here we asked to choose between four options for how they viewed Jesus:

1. He didn't exist
2. He was a real person but not divine
3. He was a real person and divine
4. He was a real person and divine and the son of God.

(Options 3 and 4 may seem to be too close, but they represented an attempt to ask a similar question in different language.) Two of these options dominated the responses, with the very large majority of respondents saying he was either "real but not divine," or that he was "real, divine, and the son of God." This revealed a trend in the research that the divisive issue at hand was not that of Jesus' existence, but of his divinity, as almost all respondents at least believed in the historical accounts of Jesus' life. One respondent mused that another option could be included in the question:

> What do you mean perfect? He can't be perfect, human nature means we can't be perfect. Is there another option: semi-perfect?

## Claims to Be the Son of God

The question that asked what respondents thought of Jesus Christ's own claims that he was the Son of God was far more divisive than the questions merely asking about his nature, with most respondents answering either firmly in favor of or against this view. Several responses considered Jesus' claims to be reasonably coextensive with the claims of the Bible generally, arguing that anyone who believed in one would effectively have to believe in both:

> *I think it's fine that Jesus claimed to be the Son of God.*

> *I don't think it's farfetched at all. If you do have that religious side to you, and you do believe in the Jesus of the Bible, it seems quite logical that he would be the Son of God.*

Most respondents, however, did not believe Jesus' claim to be the Son of God, for a host of reasons. The diversity of reasons for denying Jesus' claims was in and of itself a noteworthy feature of the responses, as it was one of the few times in the survey that there was such little similarity in the arguments given by respondents for their beliefs. The reasons included:

A. The inability to fathom his supernatural birth:

> *The Virgin Mary claim is implausible.*

B. Not being able to make sense of how such a claim could be possible:

> *It doesn't make sense, so I can't believe it.*

C. Not agreeing that the biblical account is correct:

> *I'm not even sure that he actually made those claims.*

D. And simply believing that Jesus was mistaken:

> *He wasn't a lunatic or a liar, he was just wrong.*

## Asking Big Questions

### Miracles

Another controversial question asked was whether respondents thought that Jesus performed miracles while he was alive on earth. As with the question on Jesus' claim to being the Son of God, this issue strongly divided the respondents. A minority of respondents had little or no trouble at all believing that miracles happened:

> Yes. I believe in miracles.

> Miracles give us faith in God's action in our own lives, like for healing.

Some balanced their acceptance of the idea of miracles with their reasons for still remaining partly incredulous to them.

> Not all of them, but I definitely believe that a lot of them did.

> I believe they happened but not necessarily in the way we've been told.

Nonetheless, most respondents couldn't accept the idea of supernatural occurrences taking place in a natural world, and so gave reasons for disbelieving.

> There must have been other variables. They were probably flukes or stunts.

> I don't believe in miracles. I've never seen them, so I don't agree.

> People just believe what they want to believe.

### Death on the Cross

When respondents were asked to comment on whether they believed that Jesus was crucified, the range of responses was brought back within the realm of consensus, with almost all the respondents believing that it definitely happened. Naturally there was some dissent, as with most of these questions, though the reasons for these beliefs were relatively obscure.

> *I don't believe he died on a cross. I think he was put on a stake.*
>
> *The crucifixion wasn't literal; it was a metaphor for crisis and despair.*

Among those who believed that Jesus died on the cross, beliefs varied widely, with each response adding a distinct character to what might otherwise have appeared to be a straightforward question of facts. Some focused on the reasons they believed, citing either educational upbringing or commonsense.

> *I do believe it happened. But probably just because at school they taught it to us like there was no option, it was always "This is what happened."*
>
> *It makes sense because at the time that's how they dealt with people who were threatening. He was just one of many who died on the cross. He wasn't necessarily that different.*

Meanwhile, other respondents focused less on the tenability of the claim itself, and more on their own emotional response to it, perhaps reflecting this current generation's keen interest in human rights and justice:

> *It just shows that people were barbaric.*
>
> *I think it was barbaric. He came to die for us, and it was all in vain.*

## Resurrection

The question of Jesus' resurrection was once again more divisive, being a less popular belief among the respondents than the belief that he died on the cross. This confirms a trend in this survey where respondents have been more inclined to agree with claims that don't require a supernatural explanation than those that do. Some respondents did believe or were trying to believe that Jesus was resurrected.

> *Yes, I believe it happened.*

> *I struggle to believe in the resurrection, but I try.*

However, the majority of respondents did not agree that Jesus was resurrected, with some giving a flat answer rejecting the claim without comment.

> *I guess he was crucified, but I don't believe in the rebirth.*

> *I think it happened, but not the resurrection.*

> *I don't think it happened.*

> *No.*

And with others going further, justifying their inability to accept that claim—for instance, by citing the rebuttal claim that the resurrection was a conspiracy or fraud—and even noting their own internal battle with the question, showing a remarkable honesty and readiness to admit that their opinions were still continually being formed.

> *I don't believe he was taken away by a greater entity, but by his followers.*

> *I struggle with that but I can also understand why people think it happened.*

*Qualitative Research and Interpretation*

## Implications

It almost goes without saying that this topic is by far the most important, and the pinnacle to which all the others were building.

The very positive side of this result is that most people believe in the historicity of Jesus of Nazareth, though not of everything the Bible records of him, and of his death on the cross. This gives us a huge advantage over missionaries to many countries!

Obviously the challenge is that, as in Athens, some are still mocking at the resurrection and other miraculous claims.

Strategically, we would be wise to start by building on what they already think, and putting that on an even stronger intellectual footing before then extending it. I have chosen to bridge into the topic of Jesus, which occupies the last four films, by exploring a Messianic prophecy from Daniel 9 which looks at the history of Jesus and features his death and does not strain Balmain credulity by mentioning his resurrection. It does however explain his death in terms of the gospel and atonement, not just of Roman history. This seems like sufficient extension for the first mention. A later film will take a critical look at the historicity of Jesus' resurrection, presenting as much hard evidence as possible. We will not make any claims about other miracles, but will look at his claims to divinity in the light of being resurrected. I hope this will be an effective ramp strategy.

## *Big Questions* DVD

Having surveyed people's general opinions, we also wanted their specific feedback on the first *Big Questions* film. We wanted to know what we had done right and what we could do better.

## Interesting? Entertaining?

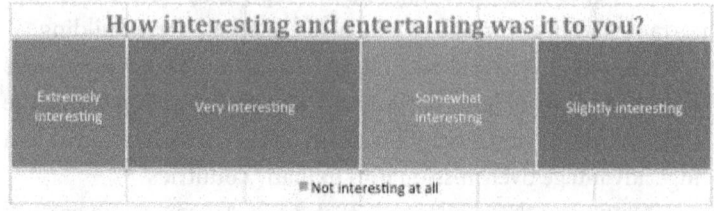

It was evident from the findings that the respondents found the DVD both interesting and entertaining, with not one choosing "not at all interesting." Overall, half expressed that they found the DVD very to extremely interesting and entertaining.

Again, given the audience, this is an encouraging result.

## Believable? Compelling?

While a good proportion of respondents found the DVD entertaining, this did not necessarily mean that everyone felt that the message of the documentary was compelling and believable. While a majority found the documentary compelling to some extent, with more than half indicating that it was extremely to very compelling, several respondents indicated that the documentary was not compelling to them at all.

One can hardly expect a half-hour documentary to change the opinions of well-educated people, especially long-term atheists and agnostics, but our aim is that will watch more and begin to question. We are aiming to make a cumulative case.

## Enjoyable and influential?

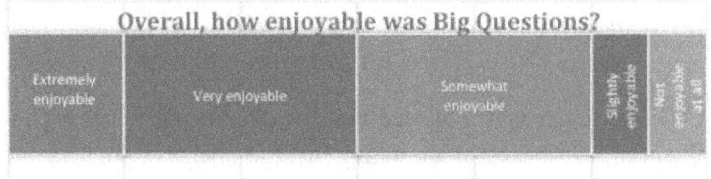

Overall, respondents found *Big Questions* quite enjoyable to watch, with half of all respondents indicated that the documentary was very to extremely enjoyable. Only a couple of respondents expressed that they found the documentary not enjoyable at all, or only slightly enjoyable.

However, while respondents found *Big Questions* entertaining, enjoyable and compelling to some extent, when asked whether the documentary influenced their worldviews, just over half stated that it did, but only to some extent. For these participants, while the documentary didn't cause them to seriously reconsider and question their beliefs, it did cause them to think about and consider their beliefs.

> It does make me think more about whether there could be a god or creator.

> It makes one think that there could be an engineer designer behind everything.

> I guess I have never really thought about how nature is how it is. [I'm] just believing God created (everything) in perfection…

> Through the medium of a documentary, it provided a lot of information about design elements within nature. I did not feel as though it was forcing you to believe on side of the debate. It provided a balanced view on possible reasons why this may be. The evidence provided and the professors who were interviewed really made me consider my beliefs and question what I thought of design.

## Asking Big Questions

> *It is easy to get caught up in everyday life and "Big Questions" reminds us that there is more at play.*

> *The section on the aerodynamics of the wings especially made me question more how everything was created.*

Just under half indicated that the documentary had not influenced their beliefs at all, stating that their beliefs were firm and unlikely to be changed. However, there was a general appreciation for the documentary and the issues it raised.

> *It triggered thoughts in me about God, but didn't change my beliefs as such.*

> *Although it raised interesting questions about the capabilities of the albatross, it did absolutely nothing in its attempts to actually answer the fundamental question.*

> *It will take more than one half hour documentary to influence my beliefs, but I always enjoy hearing different theories and points of view.*

> *It is very difficult to change my beliefs.*

### Implications

Again, one would not expect major worldview change after half an hour. Realistically, I am happy that some of the participants are beginning to question.

## Follow-On Viewing?

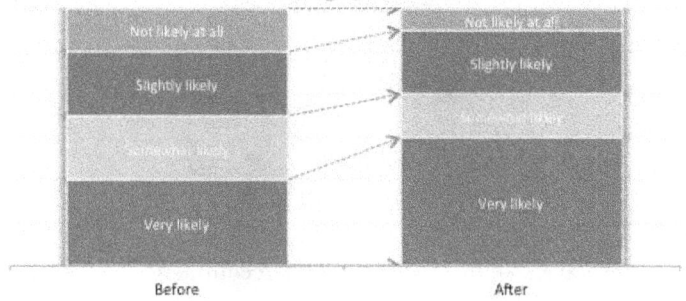

This question about future intentions to repeat business was quite encouraging, and fits with our "cumulative case" strategy, because the findings showed a discernible change in their likelihood of watching similar documentaries in the future. Before watching the documentary, there was a skew toward a lower probability of watching a similar documentary, with only a third indicating that they would be very likely to watch something like *Big Questions*. However, after watching the documentary, half of all respondents stated that they would be very likely to watch something similar to *Big Questions*.

# Asking Big Questions

## Recommend to Friends?

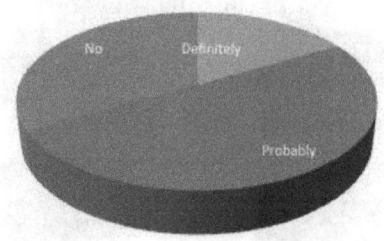

Several stated that they would not recommend the documentary to their friends, but overall, a majority of respondents indicated that they would recommend *Big Questions* to their friends.

The most effective form of film marketing, as for other kinds of marketing, is word-of-mouth recommendation. The fact that a majority of a Balmain audience—hardly Sunday School teachers—would recommend this to their friends is most encouraging.

## Detailed Feedback: Positives

Respondents were asked to comment on the sections of the documentary that they liked, and also worked well. The most common reference was to the design of the albatross wing, as well as the comparisons made with the planes.

> I enjoyed the parts that talked about the engineering of the bird's wing and how the feathers worked. That was really quite interesting.

> The explanation of how detailed the workings of a bird are, with the different aspects required to make flight possible. And also how the albatross has a built in (destination) mechanism, so it can fly very long distances.

## Qualitative Research and Interpretation

> *The comparison of man-made "birds" vs. God's was my favourite as it emphasised, albeit subtly, the differences of our creations with God's.*

> *I really enjoyed the part showed at the interview about nature's engineering of the bird wing (!)*

> *Again the workings of the bird and how man has and is still using and adapting the technology that birds use for flight.*

> *I think the link to birds and aeroplanes was quite clever, it was well streamed.*

> *The scene which had them testing out aeroplanes and design models. It was great to see how they applied the theory & knowledge they had.*

The interviews and discussions with the various academics and specialists also worked well and were also commonly mentioned by respondents.

> *The commercial planes and differing views from professors.*

> *The commentary was really interesting because they interviewed people who are specialists in their field.*

One respondent commented on that narration and commentary style of the documentary, expressing that it was both engaging and non-threatening.

> *I think the personal (nature) of the documentary works really well; for the most part, it is not simply a narration, but a person actually talking to a responder, creating a sense of intimacy and closeness.*

## Detailed Feedback: Room for Improvement

Notably, several participants indicated that nothing needed to be changed in the documentary, stating that it was a very well made production which fulfilled the purpose of informing without imposing.

> Nothing really, I think everything in the documentary was needed to explain the whole concept of the birds way of flight and man's attempt to emulate them.

When it came to areas for improvement, respondents most commonly expressed that at some points of the documentary, they felt that the pace was too slow or confusing and thus it was easy to become disengaged during those times.

> I thought that it was a bit slow moving, it took a while to get the show flowing / gain momentum. I was really quite bored at the beginning and hoped that it would get better (Which it did eventually). I also thought the places where the film was set was a bit average and very honestly, that is part of the reason I got so bored.

> It did seem to drag on a bit maybe because it's not something I would normally be interested in.

> Although I understand the necessity of a lot of the interviews, I found them, especially toward the end, to be slow and unentertaining.

> In some scenes there were too many professors being interviewed. Scenes would keep cutting and I lost track of the debate.

It was also noted that the motive of the documentary was not apparent, and was an aspect that one respondent did not enjoy.

> I didn't like that the message behind the documentary was lightly veiled.

## Qualitative Research and Interpretation

Interestingly, one of the more intellectually-driven respondents did not enjoy the documentary and the ideas and purposes behind it. For this respondent, the interviews with specialists and academics were not satisfactory, with a general feeling that the interviewees were not suitable intellectuals for the topics covered in the documentary.

> *The most annoying part that I would like to change is the comparison he makes to the albatross with model planes. It's like trying to compare an F1-Racing car to a V8 Car and a 3 year old kid riding a bike. Each item was designed for different conditions. Engineering always improves with time. I would also change the line up of "academics"...If I want an expert opinion on mathematics, I seek a mathematician, on physics, I seek a physicist, an albatross's amazing capabilities of flight—I expect a lineup of evolutionary biologists specialising in bird evolution. Not one or two engineers.*

I find it fascinating that this critical quote states that birds were designed, though I wonder if the respondent really meant that.

## Other Potential Topics of Interest

Below were some topics expressed by respondents as potential areas for further the *Big Questions* series:

**Birth** **space universe** fashion brain function creation carbon pollution and earth the human body **animals** Drug abuse solar system alcohol abuse dinosaurs insects death

## Asking Big Questions

It was noticeable that respondents had an avid interest in science and nature, with the complexities of animals, insects and plants mentioned as areas which would highly interest them.

> Ants, bees and most insects and animals really, if the series would be as thorough as this one in detailing the complexities of individual insects and animals.

> Other animals and matter that could be considered not being developed through evolution.

> Adaptation? One of the big counters of religion nowadays… is the concept of evolution, so if there were an episode of how animals were specifically designed (similarly to the feathers of the albatross) to emphasise how God not only created the environment but the harmony of the animals that can coexist even in its extreme conditions, it could be very convincing. Animals are a topic that can be seen as very friendly and light-hearted, especially towards younger children, so definitely developing on this theme could have many substantial impacts.

Other topics mentioned were those referring to creation and the universe:

> The creation of the universe or about space etc. I think humans in general are curious creatures, and topics such as those mentioned are very thought provoking and really do make you question religion / God / how it all began…

As well as more philosophical topics,

> Beginning of time…"I think therefore I am" and "the man in the machine" etc.

## Implications

Detailed feedback of this kind is very useful in fine-tuning the rest of the series. One need not follow it slavishly: for example, the person who finds the interviewees under-qualified seems to miss the point that these are leaders from both camps and Oxford professors. What

## Qualitative Research and Interpretation

greater qualification could one want? However, some find flat spots during the interviews at the end. We did leave some of the heavier, more abstract and propositional discussion for the end, reasoning that some people may switch off before then but should have the basic point; in future we should perhaps spread the propositions more evenly among the action. We should also make sure we start at full speed: for example, introduce an intriguing location or animal to promise stimulation and *then* ask the introductory thesis question of the episode.

Other respondents also take deep issue with the core argument, and may never change their minds: this is reality. However a number of comments suggest that the bird's wing detail really captivated people, and that they would be interested in more nature-based topics in future. This is useful affirmation that using nature and the awe it generates is an effective strategy.

# 5

# Conclusion

SUBJECTIVELY AT LEAST, THIS study has been worthwhile for me. In the middle of the intense process of trying to think up the best approaches to scripting a series, it offered me input from other minds and space for thought and theorizing in the midst of frantic practice. It has more than repaid any time it has taken from my work.

I have dug into the theological basis for the *Big Questions* outreach, trying to develop and nuance the theology inherent in Paul's approach in Athens. His versatility in handling different demographics has been exemplary, and his excellence in the rhetoric of the day has motivated a drive for excellence in the film medium with its own complex visual rhetoric. His ability to build bridges to the major philosophies of his day and with the arts they inspired, and to show common ground while also persuading and confronting with his worldview has generated ideas in today's culture. The apostle's equanimity at being called a seed-picking sparrow has been encouraging when atheists and agnostics, including friends on my film crew, give me *that* look, suggesting I am an ignorant faith-head. Having been a fool for lesser things in the past, I am happy to be considered a fool for Christ—though I do not want actually to be one. Paul's respect for pagan culture, and expectation that God will be active even in it, is admirable, as is his faithfulness

## Conclusion

to Scripture and the revealed religion of Christianity, and his unwillingness to leave pagans with their best guesses, but to challenge them to step up to accept God's revelation in Christ, and the gospel of counter-intuitive grace which was hidden and mysterious to many of the greatest minds. Paul's confrontation of the imagery and idolatry of the pagans has strong resonance for a filmmaker today. Paul's key themes of creation, human nature and the bodily resurrection of Jesus after his atoning death for the world must be the point to which this whole film series drives.

It was useful, if depressing, to see the decline of Christianity in Sydney (at least as measured by affiliation), and the few bright patches, and to try to analyze why this is occurring and what can be done about it. Reading this material, I related to the story of Nehemiah during his horseback reconnaissance of another city by night, seeing the walls broken down and silently scheming restoration. It was useful also to hear from people in the unsure middle, wondering about God—but not wondering very hard, as they go about their lives almost totally at a human level. This reinforces the difficulty of the task of spreading the gospel. It should motivate the church to put out our best efforts and energy and creative thought into this task Jesus left us, but also to realize our desperate need of God's empowering Spirit, without which the task is hopeless.

Moving into our own interviews, it was fascinating to hear people talk of spirituality as a vague concept, and to wonder whether we could access that for gospel purposes. A huge insight was seeing people's intuitions and feelings pulling them toward God, but their rationality—trained by a largely secular academy and media—pulling them away, and the relative strength of rationality in their decision process. I hope we can credibly address this with a rational faith that also satisfies the human heart. It was challenging to hear how irrelevant and unimportant most people find God to the meaning and purpose of their own lives, and even in crisis and times of uncertainty, and to see our need to approach the topic of God obliquely, through other topics of interest. I found it useful to hear people's responses to arguments for and against God's existence—hell, the supernatural, pain, sexual morality, consciousness, cosmology, design, fine-tuning, and the moral argument—which firmed up our topic choice and also suggested ways of approaching teach topic. I was interested too in perceptions of believers and unbelievers, which informed our choice of language. People's perceptions of Jesus were encouraging in that they know something about him (unlike most of Paul's Athens audience, and many people alive today) but challenging in how little of his supernatural nature they will accept. I must admit this gives me a strong emotional reaction, which I imagine may be something similar to Paul's own. Audience feedback on the first film was overwhelmingly encouraging, and also offered some suggested improvements. All in all, I believe this study has helped me to target my gospel communication—though time will tell how useful *Big Questions* is in growing the church.

Of course there is much more research that I wish I had time and budget to complete. My weakest findings are on the sexuality topic, and I would like to do at least a few more in-depth interviews, based on better-targeted and deeper questions. Each of the other areas could also benefit from a full study of their own.

I will leave it to others to judge whether this study is useful to them, but I would hope it may offer some insights to others who want to focus their ministry to the Balmain Tribe or equivalent in other cities, because it is arguably the leading edge of post-Christianity in this country. I would welcome robust critiques and improvements, both theoretical and practical, from anyone who is praying and working for this demographic.

I hope this study may be at least suggestive to apologists in other countries. While one would expect there to be differences across cultures, the Balmain tribe is in some ways an international class of knowledge workers, and so some insights may be applicable elsewhere on the planet.

If Christians can understand agnostics and atheists better, and have some insight into their feelings, reasoning processes, experiences and motivations, then hopefully we can more readily enter into genuine dialogue with them and prevent miscommunication. I have often been frustrated that people of faith and of no

*Conclusion*

faith often talk past each other, addressing issues that they think are issues for "the other side" rather than really listening first. It would be great to see this change.

I would certainly be interested to see this type of study into other "Tribes," and to compare results on various issues. I would hope that market research becomes standard practice as part of a strategy of applied apologetics for Christian outreach efforts, and that we can share it across denominational or traditional lines. I believe gospel communication would be better targeted as a result.

# Bibliography

Adams, Phillip. "OK, Adams, What *Do* You Believe?" In *Adams vs. God: The Rematch*, 156–62. Carlton: Melbourne University Press, 2007.
Adams, Robert M. *Finite and Infinite Goods*. New York: Oxford University Press, 1999.
———. "Flavors, Colors and God." In *Contemporary Perspectives on Religious Epistemology*, edited by R. Douglas Geivett, 225–40. New York: Oxford University Press, 1992.
———. "Moral Arguments for Theistic Belief." Chapter 10 of *The Virtue of Faith and Other Essays in Philosophical Theology*. New York: Oxford University Press, 1987.
———. "Prospects for a Metaethical Argument for Theism: A Response to Stephen J. Sullivan." *Journal of Religious Ethics* 21 (1993) 313–18.
Alston, William. "Response to Zagzebski." Chapter 14 of *Perspectives on the Philosophy of William P. Alston*, edited by Heather D. Battaly and Michael P. Lynch. Lanham, MD: Rowman & Littlefield, 2005.
Aristotle. *Rhetoric*. Translated W. Rhys Roberts. Mineola, NY: Dover, 2004.
Armstrong, John Malcolm. "Religious Attendance and Affiliation Patterns in Australia 1966 to 1996: The Dichotomy of Religious Identity and Practice." PhD diss., Australian National University, 2001. https://digitalcollections.anu.edu.au/bitstream/1885/46053/6/02whole.pdf.
Australian Bureau of Statistics. *Sydney: A Social Atlas*. Canberra: ABS, 2006.
Bahnsen, Greg L. *Always Ready: Directions for Defending the Faith*. Texarkana, AR: Covenant Media Foundation, 1996.
Balch, David L. "The Areopagus Speech: An Appeal to the Stoic Historian Posidonius against Later Stoics and the Epicureans." In *Greeks, Romans, and Christians*, edited by David L. Balch et al., 52–79. Minneapolis: Fortress, 1990.
Beckwith, Francis, and Greg Koukl. *Relativism: Feet Firmly Planted in Mid-Air*. Grand Rapids: Baker, 1998.
Bellamy, John. *Why People Don't Go to Church*. Adelaide: Openbook, 1998.

# Bibliography

Bellamy, John, et al. *Profiling Australians: Social and Religious Characteristics of the Population*. Adelaide: Openbook, 2003.

Berger, Peter L. *A Rumor of Angels: Modern Society and the Rediscovery of the Supernatural*. Garden City, NY: Doubleday, 1969.

Blaiklock, E. M. "The Areopagus Address." *Faith and Thought* 93 (1964) 175–91.

Bolt, Peter G. "New Testament Apologetics." In *New Dictionary of Christian Apologetics*, edited by W. C. Campbell-Jack et al., 487–90. Leicester, UK: InterVarsity, 2006.

Borer, Michael Ian. "The New Atheism and the Secularization Thesis." In *Religion and the New Atheism: A Critical Appraisal*, edited by in Amarnath Amarasingam, 125–37. Leiden: Brill, 2010.

Bouma, Gary D. *Australian Soul: Religion and Spirituality in the Twenty-First Century*. Melbourne: Cambridge University Press, 2006.

———. "The Emergence of Religious Plurality in Australia: A Multicultural Society." *Sociology of Religion* 56 (1995) 285–302.

Bruce, F. F. *The Book of the Acts*. Grand Rapids: Eerdmans, 1988.

———. "Paul and the Athenians." *Expository Times* 78 (1976–77) 8–12.

Burnley, Ian H. *The Impact of Immigration on Australia*. South Melbourne: Oxford University Press, 2001.

———. "Sydney's Changing Peoples: Local Expressions of Diversity and Difference." In *Talking about Sydney: Population, Community and Culture in Contemporary Sydney*, edited by Robert Freestone et al., 37–49. Sydney: University of New South Wales Press, 2006.

Burns, Alvin C., and Ronald F. Bush. *Marketing Research*. 3rd ed. Upper Saddle River, NJ: Prentice Hall, 2000.

Byrne, Peter. "Moral Arguments for the Existence of God." In *Stanford Encyclopedia of Philosophy*, no pages. First published 25 May 2004, substantive revision 4 December 2007. http://plato.stanford.edu/entries/moral-arguments-god.

Caldwell, Jill, and Christopher Brown. *Eight Tribes: The Hidden Classes of New Zealand*. Auckland: Wicked Little Books, 2009.

Carson, D. A. "Athens Revisited." In *Telling the Truth: Evangelizing Postmoderns*, edited by D. A. Carson, 384–98. Grand Rapids: Zondervan, 2000.

———. *The Gagging of God: Christianity Confronts Pluralism*. Leicester, UK: Apollos, 1996.

———. *How Long, O Lord? Reflections on Suffering & Evil*. Grand Rapids: Baker, 1990.

———. "Preaching That Understands the World." In *When God's Voice Is Heard: Essays on Preaching Presented to Dick Lucas*, edited by Christopher Green and David Jackman, 145–160. Leicester, UK: InterVarsity, 1995.

Carson, D. A., and J. D. Woodbridge. *Letters along the Way: A Novel of the Christian Life*. Wheaton, IL: Crossway, 1993.

Charles, J. Daryl. "Engaging the (Neo)Pagan Mind: Paul's Encounter with Athenian Culture as a Model for Cultural Apologetics (Acts 17:16–34)." *Trinity Journal* 16 (1995) 47–62.

# Bibliography

Chase, F. H. *The Credibility of Acts: Being the Hulsean Lectures for 1900-1901*. London, 1902. Reprint, Eugene, OR: Wipf & Stock, 2005.

Churchill, Gilbert A., Jr. *Marketing Research: Methodological Foundations*. 7th ed. Fort Worth, TX: Dryden, 1999.

Clark, David K., and Norman L. Geisler. *Apologetics in the New Age: A Christian Critique of Pantheism*. Grand Rapids: Baker, 1990.

Clark, Kelly James. "How Real People Believe: Reason and Belief in God." In *Science and Religion in Dialogue*, edited by Melville Y. Stewart, 1:481-99. Malden, MA: Wiley-Blackwell, 2010.

Collins, Paul. "Australians Quietly Spiritual, Not Godless." *Eureka Street*, 15 May 2007. http://www.eurekastreet.com.au/article.aspx?aeid=2612#.U1F7ReZdU7k.

Conifer, Steven J. "The Argument from Consciousness Refuted (2001)." No pages. www.infidels.org/library/modern/steven_conifer/ac.html.

Connell, John. "Hillsong: A Megachurch in the Sydney Suburbs." *Australian Geographer* 36 (2005) 7-22.

Conzelmann, H. "The Address of Paul on the Areopagus." In *Studies in Luke-Acts*, edited by Leander E. Keck and J. Louis Martyn, 217-30. Nashville: Abingdon, 1966.

Cook, E. David. *Blind Alley Beliefs*. 2nd ed. Leicester, UK: InterVarsity, 1996.

Cox, Harvey G. *The Secular City: Secularization and Urbanization in Theological Perspective*. New York: Macmillan, 1965.

Craig, William Lane. *Reasonable Faith: Christian Truth and Apologetics*. Wheaton, IL: Crossway, 2008.

Craig-Lees, Margaret, et al. *Consumer Behaviour*. Brisbane: Wiley, 1995.

Croft, Steven, et al. *Evangelism in a Spiritual Age: Communicating Faith in a Changing Culture*. London: Church House, 2005.

Crouch, Andy. *Culture Making: Recovering Our Creative Calling*. Downers Grove: InterVarsity, 2008.

Croy, Clayton. "Hellenistic Philosophies and the Preaching of the Resurrection (Acts 17:18, 32)." *Novum Testamentum* 39 (1997) 21-39.

Cusack, Carole M. "Some Recent Trends in the Study of Religion and Youth." *Journal of Religious History* 35 (2011) 409-18.

Dahle, Lars. "Acts 17 as an Apologetic Model." *Whitefield Briefing* 7.1 (2002) 1-4. http://klice.co.uk/uploads/whitfield/Vol%207.1%20Dahle.pdf.

———. "Acts 17:16-34: An Apologetic Model Then and Now?" *Tyndale Bulletin* 53 (2002) 313-16.

———. "Acts 17:16-34: An Apologetic Model Then and Now?" Unpublished PhD diss., Open University, UK, 2001. Provided by the author.

———. "An Apologetic Approach to the Media: Critical Christian Reflections on the Content and Form of the Media." Booklet. Kristiansand: Gimlekollen School of Journalism and Communication, 2000.

———. "Enabling Christian Media Teachers in a Convergent, Postmodern World." Booklet. Kristiansand: Gimlekollen School of Journalism and Communication, 2000.

## Bibliography

———. "Encountering and Engaging a Post-modern Context: Applying the Apologetic Model in Acts 17." *Whitefield Briefing* 7.6 (2002) 1–4. http://klice.co.uk/uploads/whitfield/Vol%207.6%20Dahle.pdf.

Dalton, Russell W. "'Electronic Areopagus': Communicating the Gospel in Multimedia Culture." *Journal of Theology* 103 (1999) 17–33.

Darwin, Charles. *The Voyage of the Beagle*. London: Everyman, 1959.

Dawkins, Richard. *The God Delusion*. Boston: Houghton Mifflin, 2008.

Deissman, Gustav Adolf. *Light from the Ancient East: The New Testament Illustrated by Recently Discovered Texts of the Graeco-Roman World*. Translated by L. R. M. Strachan. London: Hodder & Stoughton, 1910.

Demarest, Bruce A. *General Revelation: Historical Views and Contemporary Issues*. Grand Rapids: Zondervan, 1982.

Demarest, Bruce A. "General and Special Revelation: Epistemological Foundations of Religious Pluralism." In *One God, One Lord in a World of Religious Pluralism*, edited by A. D. Clarke and B. W. Winter, 135–52. Cambridge: Tyndale, 1991.

Dibelius, M. *Studies in the Acts of the Apostles*. New York: Scribner, 1956.

DiCello, C. C. "The Athenian Challenge: Lessons from Acts 17:16–34." *Darkness to Light*, 1998, no pages. http://www.dtl.org/apologetics/article/athenian.htm.

Downing, F. Gerald. "Common Ground with Paganism in Luke and in Josephus." *New Testament Studies* 28 (1982) 546–59.

Drane, John. *What Is the New Age Still Saying to the Church?* London: HarperCollins, 1999.

Dyrness, William A. *Christian Apologetics in a World Community*. Downers Grove: InterVarsity, 1983.

Earman, John. "Bayes, Hume and Miracles." *Faith and Philosophy* 10 (1993) 293–310.

———. *Hume's Abject Failure: The Argument against Miracle*. Oxford: Oxford University Press, 2000.

Edgar, William. "Two Christian Warriors: Cornelius Van Til and Francis A. Schaeffer Compared." *Westminster Theological Journal* 57 (1995) 57–80.

Edwards, David L., and John R. W. Stott. *Essentials: A Liberal-Evangelical Dialogue*. London: Hodder & Stoughton, 1988.

Ellis, E. Earle. "New Testament Teaching on Hell." In *"The Reader Must Understand": Eschatology in Bible and Theology*, edited by K. E. Brower and M. W. Elliott, 198–219. Leicester, UK: Apollos, 1997.

Engebretson, Kath. *Connecting: Teenage Boys, Spirituality and Religious Education*. Strathfield, Australia: St. Paul's, 2007.

———. "'God's Got Your Back': Teenage Boys Talk about God." *International Journal of Children's Spirituality* 11 (2006) 329–45.

———. "Young People, Culture, and Spirituality: Some Implications for Ministry." *Religious Education* 98 (2003) 5–24.

Engerman, Thomas S., ed. *Thomas Jefferson and the Politics of Nature*. Notre Dame: University of Notre Dame Press, 2000.

# Bibliography

Eros Foundation. *Hypocrites: Evidence and Statistics on Child Sexual Abuse amongst Church Clergy, 1990–2000.* Canberra: Eros, 2000. http://www.deception.com.au/images/hypocrites.pdf.

Frame, Tom. *Losing My Religion: Unbelief in Australia.* Sydney: University of New South Wales Press, 2009.

Fudge, Edward William. *The Fire That Consumes: The Biblical Case for Conditional Immortality.* Carlisle: Paternoster, 1994.

Gangel, Kenneth O. "Paul's Areopagus Speech." *Bibliotheca Sacra* 127 (1970) 308–12.

Garcia, Robert K., and Nathan L. King, eds. *Is Goodness without God Good Enough: A Debate on Faith, Secularism and Ethics.* Lanham, MD: Rowman & Littlefield, 2008.

Gärtner, Bertil E. *The Areopagus Speech and Natural Revelation.* Translated by Carolyn Hannay King. Acta Seminarii Neotestamentici Upsaliensis 21. Uppsala, Sweden: Almquist & Wiksells, 1955.

Geisler, Norman L. *Baker Encyclopedia of Christian Apologetics.* Grand Rapids: Baker, 1999.

Geisler, Norman L., and Ronald M. Brooks. *When Skeptics Ask: A Handbook on Christian Evidence.* Grand Rapids: Baker, 1990.

Geivett, R. Douglas, and Gary R. Habermas, eds. *In Defense of Miracles: A Comprehensive Case for God's Action in History.* Downers Grove: InterVarsity, 1997.

Gempf, Conrad. "Before Paul Arrived in Corinth: The Mission Strategies in 1 Corinthians 2:2 and Acts 17." In *The New Testament in Its First Century Setting: Essays on Context and Background*, edited by P. J. Williams et al., 126–42. Cambridge: Eerdmans, 2004.

Gerstner, John H. *Repent or Perish: With a Special Reference to the Conservative Attack on Hell.* Morgan, PA: Soli Deo Gloria, 1996.

Gillezeau, Marcus. *Hands On: A Practical Guide to Production and Technology in Film, TV and New Media.* Sydney: Currency, 2004.

Given, Mark D. "Not Either/Or but Both/And in Paul's Areopagus Speech." *Biblical Interpretation* 3 (1995) 356–72.

Gray, Patrick. "Athenian Curiosity (Acts 17:21)." *Novum Testamentum* 47 (2005) 109–16.

———. "Implied Audiences in the Areopagus Narrative." *Tyndale Bulletin* 55 (2004) 205–18.

Green, Michael. *Acts for Today: First Century Christianity for Twentieth Century Christians.* London: Hodder & Stoughton, 1993.

———. *Evangelism in the Early Church.* London: Hodder & Stoughton, 1970.

———. *Evangelism through the Local Church.* London: Hodder & Stoughton, 1990.

Guinness, Os. *Fit Bodies, Fat Minds: Why Evangelicals Don't Think and What to Do about It.* Grand Rapids: Baker, 1994.

## Bibliography

———. "Mission in the Face of Modernity." In *The Gospel in the Modern World: A Tribute to John Stott*, edited by Martyn Eden and David Wells, 114–23. Leicester, UK: InterVarsity, 1991.

Gulley, Philip, and James Mulholland. *If Grace Is True: Why God Will Save Every Person*. San Francisco: Harper, 2004.

Haenchen, Ernst. *The Acts of the Apostles*. Translated by Bernard Noble and Gerald Shinn from the 14th ed. of *Die Apostelgeschichte*. Translation revised by R. McL. Wilson. Philadelphia: Westminster, 1971.

Hansen, G. Walter. "The Preaching and Defence of Paul." In *Witness to the Gospel: The Theology of Acts*, edited by I. Howard Marshall and David Peterson, 295–324. Grand Rapids: Eerdmans, 1998.

Hare, John E. *Moral Faith and Providence*. Paper presented at the 1996 Annual Wheaton Philosophy Conference. http://www.calvin.edu/academic/philosophy/writings/moralpro.htm.

———. *The Moral Gap: Kantian Ethics, Human Limits, and God's Assistance*. Oxford: Clarendon, 1996.

———. *Why Bother Being Good? The Place of God in the Moral Life*. Downers Grove: InterVarsity, 2002.

Harmon, Kendall S. "The Case against Conditionalism." In *Univeralism and the Doctrine of Hell: Papers Presented at the Fourth Edinburgh Conference in Christian Dogmatics, 1991*, edited by Nigel M. de S. Cameron, 193–224. Carlisle: Paternoster, 1992.

Harris, Sam. *The Moral Landscape: How Science Can Determine Human Values*. London: Bantam, 2010.

Hartnett, John W. *Starlight, Time and the New Physics: How We Can See Starlight in Our Young Universe*. Eight Mile Plains, Australia: Creation, 2007.

Head, Peter M. "The Duration of Divine Judgment in the New Testament." In *Eschatology in Bible and Theology: Evangelical Essays at the Dawn of a New Millennium*, edited by K. E. Brower and M. W. Elliott, 199–227. Downers Grove: InterVarsity, 1997.

Hemer, Colin J. "The Speeches of Acts: Pt 1: The Ephesian Elders at Miletus; Pt 2: The Areopagus Address." *Tyndale Bulletin* 40 (1989) 239–59.

Hesse, Mary. "Miracles and the Laws of Nature." In *Miracles*, edited by C. F. D. Moule. London: Mowbray, 1965.

Hitchens, Christopher. *God Is Not Great: The Case Against Religion*. London: Atlantic, 2007.

Hogan, Michael. "Australian Secularists: The Disavowal of Denominational Allegiance." *Journal for the Scientific Study of Religion* 18 (1979) 390–404.

Horsley, G. H. R. "Speeches and Dialogue in Acts." *New Testament Studies* 32 (1986) 609–14.

Hughes, Philip J., ed. *Australia's Religious Communities: A Multimedia Exploration*. 3rd ed. Nunawading, Australia: Christian Research Association, 2010.

———. "Characteristics of Religious Knowledge among Australian Students." *International Journal of Children's Spirituality* 12 (2007) 137–47.

## Bibliography

———. *Putting Life Together: Findings from Australia Youth Spirituality Research*. Fairfield: Fairfield Press, 2007.

———. *Shaping Australia's Spirituality: A Review of Christian Ministry in the Australian Context*. With contributions from Stephen Reid, and Claire Pickering. Preston, Australia: Mosaic, 2010.

———. *The True Image: The Nature and Destiny of Man in Christ*. Grand Rapids: Eerdmans, 1989.

Hughes, Philip J., and Sharon Bond. "Exploring What Australians Value." With John Bellamy and Alan Black. Research paper (Christian Research Association) 5. Adelaide: Openbook, 2003.

Jefferson, Thomas. Letter to William Short, 11 October 1819. In *Thomas Jefferson and the Politics of Nature*, edited by Thomas S. Engerman. Notre Dame: University of Notre Dame Press, 2000.

Kaldor, Peter. *Build My Church: Trends and Possibilities for Australian Churches* Sydney: Australian Church Resources, 1999.

Kaldor, Peter, Leslie J. Francis, and Philip J. Hughes. "Personality and Community Involvement: Is Churchgoing Different?" *Journal of Beliefs & Values* 23 (2002) 101–5.

Kaldor, Peter, Philip Hughes, and Alan Black. *Spirit Matters: How Making Sense of Life Affects Wellbeing*. Melbourne: Mosaic, 2010.

Kent, Grenville J. R. *Big Questions Prospectus*. Self published, 2010.

———. "Pop Culture: My Angel Goes to Movies." In *Unleash the Dream: A Generation Challenges the Church They Love*, edited by Andy Nash, 52–62. Hagerstown, MD: Review & Herald, 1999.

———. *Say It Again, Sam: A Literary and Filmic Study of Narrative Repetition in 1 Samuel 28*. Eugene, OR: Pickwick, 2011.

King, Nigel, and Christine Horrocks. *The Qualitative Research Interview*. London: Sage, 2010.

Langmead, Ross. "Not Quite Established: The Gospel and Australian Culture." *Gospel and Our Culture* 14 (2002) 7–10.

———, ed. *Reimagining God and Mission: Perspectives from Australia*. Adelaide: ATF, 2007.

———. "Theological Reflection in Ministry and Mission." *Ministry Society and Theology* 18 (2004) 9–28.

———. *The Word Made Flesh: Towards an Incarnational Missiology*. American Society of Missiology Dissertation Series. Lanham, MD: University Press of America, 2004.

Layman, C. Stephen. "God and the Moral Order." *Faith and Philosophy* 19 (2002) 304–16.

———. "God and the Moral Order: Replies to Objections." *Faith and Philosophy* 23 (2006) 209–12.

———. "A Moral Argument for the Existence of God." In *Is Goodness without God Good Enough: A Debate on Faith, Secularism and Ethics*, edited by Robert K. Garcia and Nathan L. King, 49–66. Lanham, MD: Rowman & Littlefield, 2008.

## Bibliography

Legrand, L. "The Areopagus Speech: Its Theological Kerygma and Its Missionary Significance." In *La Notion de Dieu*, edited by J. Coppens, 338–41. Louvain: Gembloux, 1974.

Lewis, C. S. *Miracles: A Preliminary Study*. New York: Harper, 1947.

Linville, Mark. "The Moral Argument." In *The Blackwell Companion to Natural Theology*, edited by William Lane Craig and J. P. Moreland, 393–417. Oxford: Blackwell, 2009.

Litwak, Kenneth D. "Israel's Prophets Meet Athens' Philosophers: Scriptural Echoes in Acts 17, 22–31." Biblica 85 (2004) 199–216.

Lohrey, Amanda. "Voting for Jesus: Christianity and Politics in Australia." *Quarterly Essay* 22 (2006) 1–79.

MacDonald, Gregory. *The Evangelical Universalist*. Eugene, OR: Cascade, 2006.

Mackay, Hugh. *Advance Australia—Where?* Sydney: Hachette Livre Australia, 2007.

Maddox, Marion. *God under Howard: The Rise of the Religious Right in Australian Politics*. Crows Nest, Australia: Allen & Unwin, 2005.

Malherbe, Abraham J. *Paul and the Popular Philosophers*. Minneapolis: Fortress, 1989.

Malhotra, Naresh K. *Marketing Research: An Applied Orientation*. Sydney: Prentice Hall, 1996.

Marshall, I. Howard. *The Acts of the Apostles: An Introduction and Commentary*. Grand Rapids: Eerdmans, 1980.

Mason, Michael, et al. *The Spirit of Generation Y: Young People's Spirituality in a Changing Australia*. Mulgrave, Australia: Garratt, 2007.

Mayers, Ronald B. *Balanced Apologetics: Using Evidences and Presuppositions in Defense of the Faith*. Grand Rapids: Kregel, 1984.

McCrindle, Mark. *Emerging Trends, Enduring Truth: The Spiritual Attitudes of the New Generations*. Sydney: McCrindle Research, 2009.

McCrindle, Mark, and Emily Wolfinger. *The ABC of XYZ: Understanding the Global Generations*. Sydney: University of New Sout Wales Press, 2009.

McGrath, Alister E. "Biblical Models for Apologetics, Part 1: Evangelical Apologetics." *Bibliotheca Sacra* 155 (1998) 3–10.

———. "Biblical Models for Apologetics, Part 2: Apologetics to the Jews." *Bibliotheca Sacra* 155 (1998) 131–38.

———. "Biblical Models for Apologetics, Part 3: Apologetics to the Greeks." *Bibliotheca Sacra* 155 (1998) 259–65.

———. "Biblical Models for Apologetics, Part 4: Apologetics to the Romans." *Bibliotheca Sacra* 155 (1998) 387–93.

———. *Bridge-Building: Effective Christian Apologetics*. Leicester, UK: InterVarsity, 1992.

———. "The Challenge of Pluralism for the Contemporary Church." *Journal of the Evangelical Theological Society* 35 (1992) 361–73.

———. *The NIV Bible Companion*. London: Hodder & Stoughton, 1995.

———. *A Passion for Truth: The Intellectual Coherence of Evangelicalism*. Leicester, UK: Apollos, 1996.

## Bibliography

———. *The Unknown God: Searching for Spiritual Fulfilment.* Oxford: Lion, 1999.
McGrath, Alister. E., and Michael Green. *Springboard for Faith.* London: Hodder & Stoughton, 1993.
McKay, Kenneth L. "Foreign Gods Identified in Acts 17:18." *Tyndale Bulletin* 45 (1994) 411–12.
Montgomery, John Warwick. *Faith Founded on Fact: Essays in Evidential Apologetics.* Nashville: Nelson, 1978.
Moreland, J. P. "The Argument from Consciousness." In *The Rationality of Theism*, edited by Paul Copan and Paul Moser, 204–20. London: Routledge, 2003.
Netland, H. A. "Apologetics, Worldviews, and the Problem of Neutral Criteria." *Trinity Journal* 12 (1991) 39–58.
Newbigin, Lesslie. *Foolishness to the Greeks: The Gospel and Western Culture.* London: SPCK, 1986.
Nowak, Martin. *Super Cooperators: Evolution, Altruism and Human Behaviour; or, Why We Need Each Other to Succeed.* Melbourne: Text, 2011.
Oliphint, K. Scott. *The Battle Belongs to the Lord: The Power of Scripture for Defending the Faith.* Phillipsburg, NJ: Presbyterian & Reformed, 2003.
Onfray, Michel. *The Atheist Manifesto: The Case against Christianity, Judaism and Islam.* Translated by Jeremy Leggatt. Melbourne: Melbourne University Press, 2007. First published as *Traité d'Athéologie*, Éditions Grasset & Fasquelle, 2005.
Packer, J. I. "Evangelical Annihilationism in Review." *Reformation & Revival* 6 (1997) 37–51.
———. "Evangelicals and the Way of Salvation: New Challenges to the Gospel." In *Evangelical Affirmations*, edited by Kenneth S. Kantzer and Carl F. H. Henry, 107–36. Grand Rapids: Zondervan, 1990.
Pao, David W. *Acts and the Isaianic New Exodus.* Tübingen: Mohr Siebeck, 2000.
Parente, P. "St. Paul's Address before the Areopagus." *Catholic Biblical Quarterly* 11 (1949) 144–50.
Parry, Robin A., and Christopher H. Partridge, eds. *Universal Salvation? The Current Debate.* Grand Rapids: Eerdmans, 2003.
Peterson, D. "Resurrection Apologetics and the Theology of Luke-Acts." In *Proclaiming the Resurrection: Papers from the First Oak Hill College Annual School of Theology*, edited by Peter M. Head, 29–57. Carlisle: Paternoster, 1998. See also http://davidgpeterson.com/acts/resurrection-and-luke-acts.
Peterson, Robert A. *Hell on Trial: The Case for Eternal Punishment.* Phillipsburg, NJ: Presbyterian & Reformed, 1995.
Pinnock, Clark H. "The Destruction of the Finally Impenitent." *Journal from the Radical Reformation* 2 (1992) 4–21.
Plantinga, Alvin. *God, Freedom, and Evil.* Grand Rapids: Eerdmans, 1977.
Porter, Stanley E. *The Paul of Acts: Essays in Literary Criticism, Rhetoric and Theology.* Tübingen: Mohr Siebeck, 1999.

## Bibliography

Possamai, Adam. *In Search of New Age Spiritualities.* Aldershot, UK: Ashgate, 2005.

Postman, Neil. *Amusing Ourselves to Death: Public Discourse in the Age of Show Business.* New York: Viking, 1985.

Postman, Neil, and Camille Paglia. "She Wants Her TV! He Wants His Book!" *Harpers Magazine*, March 1991, 44–55.

Prior, Kenneth F. W. *The Gospel in a Pagan Society.* 2nd ed. Fearn, Scotland: Christian Focus, 1995.

Proctor, John. "The Gospel from Athens: Paul's Speech before the Areopagus and the Evangel for Today." *Evangel* 10 (1992) 69–72.

Ramsay, W. M. *St. Paul the Traveller and Roman Citizen.* London: Hodder & Stoughton, 1895.

Riddell, Michael. *Threshold of the Future: Reforming the Church in the Post-Christian West.* London: SPCK, 1998.

Robertson, Geoffrey. *The Case of the Pope: Vatican Accountability for Human Rights Abuse.* London: Penguin, 2010.

Rodenburg, Patsy. *The Need for Words: Voice and the Text.* London: Methuen, 1993.

Safranski, Rüdiger. *Schopenhauer and the Wild Years of Philosophy.* Translated by Ewald Osers. Cambridge: Harvard University Press, 1991.

Salt, Bernard. "Catholics vs. Non-believers." *Australian*, 25 March 2010.

Savage, Sarah B., et al. *Making Sense of Generation Y: The Worldview of 15- to 25-Year-Olds.* London: Church House, 2006.

Schnabel, Eckhard J. "Contextualising Paul in Athens: The Proclamation of the Gospel before Pagan Audiences in the Graeco-Roman World." *Religion & Theology* 12 (2005) 172–90.

Schroeder, Gerald L. *Genesis and the Big Bang: The Discovery of Harmony between Modern Science and the Bible.* New York: Bantam, 1990.

Stevenson, Deborah, et al. "Religious Belief across 'Post-secular' Sydney: The Multiple Trends in (De)Secularisation." *Australian Geographer* 41 (2010) 323–50.

Stonehouse, N. B. "*Paul before the Areopagus: And Other New Testament Studies.* London: Tyndale, 1957.

Storkey, Elaine. "Change and Decay in British Society?" In *The Gospel in the Modern World: A Tribute to John Stott*, edited by Martyn Eden and David Wells, 108–23. Leicester, UK: InterVarsity, 1991.

Stott, John R. W. *The Contemporary Christian: An Urgent Plea for Double Listening.* Leicester, UK: InterVarsity, 1992.

———. *The Message of Acts: To the Ends of the Earth.* Leicester, UK: InterVarsity, 1994.

Street, Sharon. "A Darwinian Dilemma for Realist Theories of Value." *Philosophical Studies* 127 (2006) 109–66.

Swinburne, Richard. "Arguments from Consciousness and Morality." Chapter 9 of *The Existence of God.* 2nd ed. Oxford: Clarendon, 1991.

———. *The Concept of Miracle.* New York: Macmillan, 1970.

———. *Miracles.* New York: Mamillan, 1989.
Tacey, David J. *Edge of the Sacred: Transformation in Australia.* Melbourne: HarperCollins, 1995.
———. *Re-enchantment: The New Australian Spirituality.* Sydney: HarperCollins, 2000.
———. *The Spirituality Revolution: The Emergence of Contemporary Spirituality.* Pymble, Autralia: HarperCollins, 2003.
———. "What Spirituality Means to Young Adults." In *Religion and Youth*, edited by Sylvia Collins-Mayo and Pink Dandelion, 65–71. Farnham, Surrey: Ashgate, 2010.
Thornton, L. R. "Paul's Apologetic at Athens and Ours." *Calvary Baptist Theological Journal* 2 (1986) 2–22.
Van Til, Cornelius. *Paul at Athens.* Phillipsburg, NJ: Presbyterian & Reformed, 1978.
Vincenzo, Joseph P. "Nietzsche and Epicurus." Man and World 27 (1994) 383–97.
Wrainwright, William. *Religion and Morality.* Aldershot: Ashgate, 2005.
Warner, R. Stephen, and Rhys H. Williams. "The Role of Families and Religious Institutions in Transmitting Faith among Christians, Muslims and Hindus in the USA." In *Religion and Youth*, edited by Sylvia Collins-Mayo and Pink Dandelion, 159–65. Surrey, UK: Ashgate, 2010.
Wenham, John W. "The Case for Conditional Immortality." In *Univeralism and the Doctrine of Hell*, edited by Nigel M. de S. Cameron, 161–91. Carlisle: Paternoster, 1992.
Whitcomb, John C., Jr. "Contemporary Apologetics and the Christian Faith. Part I: Human Limitations in Apologetics." *Bibliotheca Sacra* 134 (1977) 99–106.
Wiker, Benjamin, and Jonathan Witt. *A Meaningful World: How the Arts and Sciences Reveal the Genius of Nature.* Downers Grove: IVP Academic, 2006.
Williams, Alex, and John W. Hartnett. *Dismantling the Big Bang: God's Universe Rediscovered.* Green Forest, AR: Master, 2007.
Williams, Robyn. *Unintelligent Design: Why God Isn't as Smart as She Thinks She Is.* Crows Nest, Australia: Allen & Unwin, 2006.
Wilson, Stephen G. *The Gentiles and the Gentile Mission in Luke-Acts.* Cambridge: Cambridge University Press, 1973.
Winter, Bruce W. "In Public and in Private: Early Christian Interactions with Religious Pluralism." In *One God, One Lord in a World of Religious Pluralism*, edited by Bruce W. Winter and Andrew D. Clarke, 112–34. Cambridge: Tyndale, 1991.
———. "Introducing the Athenians to God: Paul's Failed Apologetic in Acts 17?" *Themelios* 31 (2005) 38–59.
———. "On Introducing Gods to Athens: An Alternative Reading of Acts 17:18–20." *Tyndale Bulletin* 47 (1996) 71–90.

## Bibliography

———. *Philo and Paul among the Sophists*. Cambridge: Cambridge University Press, 1997.

Wright, R. K. McGregor. "Paul's Purpose at Athens and the Problem of 'Common Ground.'" Research paper of the Aquila and Priscilla Study Centre, 1996. www.vantil.info/articles/rkmw_ppaa.pdf.

Zeolla, Gary F. "Paul in Athens: Paradigm for Modern-day Evangelism." *Darkness to Light*, 1999, no pages. http://www.dtl.org/apologetics/article/paul-athens.htm.

# Subject Index

AB demographic, 20
Abuse, 89, 108, 110
agnostic(s), 55–56, 74, 138, 148, 150
altruism, 80, 118–19, 161
Aratus, 34
Areopogitica, 38
Areopagite(s), 18, 21, 38
Areopagus, 18–19, 22, 24–27, 29, 31, 33–34, 36–37, 39, 45–46, 48–49, 88, 153–58, 160–62
Aristotle, 20–21, 154
*ataraxia*, 26
atheism, 2, 28, 55, 59, 154
atheist(s), 13, 28, 30, 48, 55–56, 58, 87–89, 91, 94, 99, 102, 109, 111, 127, 138, 148, 154, 161
atomist, 27
Audi, 20
autarkeia, 29
census, 54, 56–57, 60
Corinth, 19–21, 157

Corinthians, 19–20, 157
cosmology/cosmologist/cosmological, 5, 12, 79, 112–13, 117, 150
creation, 36, 43–45, 96, 103, 112, 117, 146, 149, 158
curiosity, xii, 4, 46, 73, 89, 92, 95, 100, 157
curious, vi, 88–89, 92, 146
Darwin, 27, 44, 117, 122, 156
Darwinian, 121, 162
Dawkins, 2, 30, 89, 99, 117, 156
design, xii, 12, 44, 79, 82, 115–17, 117, 139, 142–43, 160, 163
designed, 103, 145–46
designer, 139
Dionysian, 41
Dionysius, 21, 38
DNA, 12, 29, 79, 115
ecology, 98
economic(s /ally /ism), 45, 49, 61
Eden, 158, 162

165

## Subject Index

emotion(al), ix, 1, 21, 64, 75, 87, 89–90, 94, 100, 135, 150
emotionally, 4, 41, 87, 106, 117
Enlightenment, 45
Epicurean(ism), 13, 27–28
Epicureans(s), 24, 26–28, 45, 153
Epicurus, 26–28, 163
Epimenides, 33–34
epistemology (ical), 34, 65, 153, 156
Eros, 114, 157
eroticism, 41
eschatology, 99, 156, 158
ethnic(ity), 10, 23
Eumenides, 45
Evangelical(s), 24–25, 31, 42, 78, 99, 126, 129, 156–58, 160–61
evangelism, 1–2, 5, 15, 22, 74, 88, 99, 155, 157, 164
evangelist(s /ic), 2, 5, 17, 18, 24–25, 32, 36–37, 43, 51, 95, 126
evolution, 110–12, 116–17, 145–46, 161
evolutionary, 50, 110, 116, 121, 128, 145
evolve(d), 44, 117, 119
faith, ix, 3, 17, 21–22, 31–32, 42, 48, 40, 54, 56–57, 59–60, 63, 65, 66, 69, 84, 87–88, 92, 95, 99–103, 121, 123, 125, 127, 134, 148–51, 163

feelings, 28, 42, 75, 77, 86, 90, 92, 105, 115, 149–50
film(s), ix, xi, 1–2, 4–5, 10, 14–15, 32, 42–45, 47, 81–83, 89, 92, 94, 99, 103, 109–110, 137, 142, 144, 148–150, 157
filmmaker, 2, 28, 42, 47, 149
God, ix–x, xii–3, 5, 11, 13–15, 17, 18, 10–11, 28–30, 32–37, 39, 41, 43–48, 42–54, 56, 50–51, 63–67, 71–74, 76–80, 85–92, 94–100, 102–23, 131–34, 139–40, 143, 146, 148–49, 153–63
goddess, 38
Godless, 155
gods, 28–30, 39, 101, 161, 163
hedonist, 9, 26–27
hell, 79, 97–98, 149, 156–58, 161, 163
immortal (ity/ ised), 43, 99, 129, 157, 163
laugh(ter), 9, 927
market, ix, xi, 1–2, 4, 6, 18, 20, 22, 24–25, 30, 42, 49, 61, 82, 151
marketing, 2–3, 5, 18, 20, 24–25, 39, 51, 60, 75, 82, 142, 154–55, 160
marketplace, 24–25, 31, 42, 48–49, 74
Marx(ism), 26–27, 50
materialism/ materialist(s), 11, 13, 24, 26–27, 45, 49

## Subject Index

moral(ity), 13, 18, 43–44, 40, 66, 79–80, 94, 110, 118–22, 130–31, 150, 153–54, 158–60, 162–63
morals, 29, 108, 118–21, 130
narrative, 18, 21–22, 32, 23–24, 26, 33, 92, 157, 159
naturalism, 102
nature, xi, 11–12, 17, 26–27, 29–30, 37, 40, 43–44, 60, 66, 73–74, 79, 89, 101, 103, 115, 118, 132–33, 139, 143, 146–47, 149–50, 156, 163
Nietzsche, Friedrich, 27, 91, 163
nihilism, 27, 29
objectivists, 119
pagan(ism), 17–18, 22, 28, 36–44, 148–49, 154, 156, 162
panentheistic, 29
pantheism/ pantheistic, 29, 38, 155
postmodern, 47–49, 73, 91–92, 154–55
qualitative, 75–77, 79, 81, 83, 85, 87, 89, 91, 93, 95, 97, 99, 101, 103, 105, 107, 109, 111, 113, 115, 117, 119, 121, 123, 125, 127, 129, 131, 133, 135, 137, 139, 141, 143, 145, 147, 159
quantitative, 60, 83, 87, 113, 122
random(ness), xii, 26–28
reincarnation, 45

relativism, 46, 49–50, 73, 122, 153
religion(s), 11, 15, 33, 39, 41, 46–48, 50, 52–56, 58, 60, 65, 67, 69–70, 73, 78, 83–84, 87, 89, 98, 101, 106–7, 109, 114–15, 118, 121, 123, 127, 129–32, 146, 149, 154–55, 157–58, 162–63
Schopenhauer, Artur, 27, 162
science, 48, 50, 69, 73, 88, 102, 112–119, 121, 146, 155, 162–63
scientific, 27–28, 68, 77, 94, 97, 100, 102–3, 110, 113, 115, 117
scientism, 49
secular(ism), 13–14, 28, 49–50, 55, 60, 74, 94, 96, 111, 121–22, 127, 149, 155, 157, 159, 162
secularisation, 55–56, 59, 154–55, 162
segment(ation), ix, 6, 18, 20, 22–24, 26, 57
Seinfeld, 27
sex(uality), 13–14, 40, 94, 107–10, 149–50, 157
skepticism, 101–2, 104, 131
Skeptics, 17, 157
Sophists, 164
soul(s), xi, 13, 25, 29, 45, 55, 66, 74, 90, 109, 150
spiritual, 9, 11, 30, 40, 45–46, 54–56, 60–61, 64, 66, 70,

## Subject Index

72–74, 77, 79, 84–85, 87, 94, 101, 105, 110, 113, 116, 123, 130, 155, 160–63
spirituality, 16, 46, 52–55, 60–61, 64, 72, 74, 76, 84–85, 91, 96, 109, 115, 149, 154, 156, 158–60, 163
Stoics, 24, 29–30, 45–46, 153
story, storytelling, 22–24, 32–33, 43, 49, 96, 131, 149
theism, 3, 5, 30, 88, 92, 103, 120, 153, 161
theistic, 65, 117, 120, 153
unbelief, unbelievers, 1, 85, 92, 150, 157
universalism, 46, 99, 160
values, 6, 10–13, 50, 59, 62, 63, 66, 70–71, 118, 158–59
Whateverism, 73
Wicca, 33
worldview, 12, 17, 37, 45, 48, 74, 87, 104, 139–40, 148, 161–62

# Author Index

Adams, Phillip, 28
Adams, Douglas, 91
Adams, Robert, 111, 120–21
Allen, Woody, 27
Alston, William, 121, 153
Armstrong, John Malcolm, 54, 153
Berger, Peter L., 48, 154
Blaiklock, E.M., 19, 22, 26–27, 29, 31, 33–34, 39, 46, 154
Bouma, Gary, 54–55, 57, 154
Caldwell, Jill, ix, xi, 6–7, 59, 61, 64, 154
Collins, Paul, 55
Conzelmann, H., 18, 155
Copan, Paul, 154
Cox, Harvey G., 55, 155
Dahle, Lars, xii, 17, 21–24, 29, 33, 35–37, 44, 46–50, 155–56
Deissman, Gustav A., 27, 164
Dibelius, M., 19, 35, 156
DiCello, C.C., 17, 156
Dyrness, William A., 17, 156

Earman, John, 103, 156
Edgar, William, 14, 156
Engebretson, Kathleen, 52, 56, 92, 156
Eriksen, Berg, 49
Gärtner, Bertil, 157
Geisler, Norman L., 17, 155, 157
Geivett, R. Douglas, 103, 153, 157
Gillezeau, Marcus, 2, 157
Guinness, Os, 17, 50, 157
Hughes, Philip J., xii, 53, 73, 92, 99, 158–59
Josephus, Flavius, 12
Kaldor, Peter, 54, 159
Koukl, Greg, 122, 153
Malhotra, Naresh K., 75, 160
McGrath, Alister, 17, 19, 26, 48, 99, 160–61
Moreland, J.P., 111, 160–61
Newbigin, Lesslie, 50, 161
Onfray, Michel, 2, 109, 161
Paglia, Camille, 39–41, 43, 162
Porsche, Ferdinand, xi

*Author Index*

Postman, Neil, 31, 39–42, 162
Roberston, 108, 162
Schaeffer, Francis, 13–14, 156
Schnabel, Eckhard J., 319, 36–37, 162
Schroeder, Gerald L., 114, 162
Stevenson, Deborah, 55–60, 162
Storkey, Elaine, 49, 162
Stott, John R.W., 19–20, 99, 156, 158, 162
Wenham, John W., 99, 163
Wiker, Benjamin, 27–28, 163
Witt, Jonathan, 27–28, 163

www.ingramcontent.com/pod-product-compliance
Lightning Source LLC
Chambersburg PA
CBHW050808160426
43192CB00010B/1686